Minnesota's Forests
1999-2003 Part A

USDA Forest Service
Forest Inventory and Analysis Program
Northern Research Station, St. Paul, MN

Patrick D. Miles, Keith Jacobson, Gary J. Brand, Ed Jepsen, Dacia Meneguzzo,
Manfred E. Mielke, Cassandra Olson, Charles (Hobie) Perry, Ron Piva,
Barry Tyler Wilson, and Chris Woodall

Foreword

Minnesota sits at the crossroads of three major ecosystems—prairies to the west, boreal forests to the north, and hardwoods to the south—and its forests reflect the variety of the State's unique location.

During the late 19th and early 20th century, nearly half of Minnesota's forest land was converted to agriculture and other land uses in the wake of widespread lumbering that peaked in 1905 (Waters 1977). Since then, the history of the State's forests has been primarily one of recovery. This latest report, however, shows a slight decline in the area of forest land from 1990. Demands placed on forest resources will continue to increase along with biological threats from nonnative plants and insects. Minnesotans face this challenge: to maintain forests in such a way that they can be used and enjoyed today as well as in the future.

To know whether Minnesota's resources are being maintained in a sustainable way, we need to be able to report on trends in the condition and status of forest resources. The U.S. Department of Agriculture, Forest Service, through its Forest Inventory and Analysis program and in partnership with the Minnesota Department of Natural Resources, Division of Forestry, inventoried Minnesota's forest resources in 1935, 1953, 1962, 1977, and 1990. In 1999, the periodic inventories were changed to annual inventories in which a portion of field plots were inventoried each year and a full inventory was completed after 5 years. The first Minnesota annual inventory was completed in 2003 and covers the period 1999-2003.

In this report we attempt to briefly describe the current condition and health of Minnesota's forests. We hope the information provided will stimulate discussion about the State's forest resources and spur further research and analysis into maintaining the health and vigor of Minnesota's forests.

NOTE: Information including core tables, glossary, and sample/QA/QC methods will be included in a companion document (Part B) to be released as an Internet publication in tandem with this 5-year report. Data from the Minnesota forest inventory can be accessed electronically at: http://www.nrs.fs.fed.us/fia.

Contents

Highlights

▓ Minnesota is nearly 32 percent forest land. It ranks 14th among the 50 States in land area, 19th in forest land area, and 12th in timberland area.

▓ The number of live trees on timberland increased in Minnesota from 1977 to 2003. The number of sapling and sawtimber trees increased while the number of poletimber trees decreased.

▓ The total dry biomass of all-live trees on timberland increased from 409 million tons in 1977 to 432 million tons in 2003—a 5.6-percent increase.

▓ The volume of growing-stock trees increased from 12.3 billion cubic feet in 1977 to 15.1 billion in 1990 to 15.3 billion in 2003. The largest increases in volume were in tamarack (117-percent increase), sugar maple (95 percent), red pine (91 percent), bur oak (84 percent), and northern white-cedar (77 percent).

▓ All-live cubic foot volume per acre on timberland increased from 1,050 in 1977 to 1,082 in 1990 to 1,107 in 2003.

▓ The volume of sawtimber on timberland increased from 23.7 billion board feet in 1977 to 34.9 billion in 1990 to 38.7 billion in 2003 because of an increase in both the number and size of sawtimber trees.

▓ Average annual net growth of growing stock, over 1990-2002, was 404 million cubic feet for Minnesota. This is equivalent to 2.6 percent of the total growing-stock volume in 2003.

▓ Average annual removals of growing stock, over 1990-2002, was 249 million cubic feet for Minnesota, or roughly 1.6 percent of the total growing-stock volume in 2003.

▓ The growth to removals ratio of 1.6, for 1990 to 2003, indicates that net growth is greater than removals and that growing-stock volume is increasing.

▓ Fuel loadings of down woody materials are not exceedingly high in Minnesota compared to areas of high fire hazard in Western States.

▓ Ozone damage to forests is not significant in Minnesota.

▓ In Minnesota, for every 100 live trees more than 5 inches in diameter, 13 standing dead trees provide valuable wildlife habitat.

▓ Overall, 92 percent of the trees had no tree crown dieback, 7 percent had light dieback, and only 1 percent had moderate or severe dieback.

▓ In Minnesota, approximately 29,200 people are employed in primary processing (including logging) and 24,000 are employed in secondary manufacturing.

▓ Average annual net growth is expected to continue to exceed average annual removals over the next 50 years. The volume per acre of timberland is projected, by the national timber assessment, to increase from the current 1,035 cubic feet to 2,003 cubic feet by 2060.

- The area of forest land has decreased by 4 percent since 1990. Slightly more than 90 percent of land forested in 1990 remained forest land 12 years later. Roughly 10 percent of the forest was lost to other land uses, primarily marshland. Approximately two-thirds of this loss in forest land was offset by nonforest land, primarily marshland, reverting to forest land.

- High mortality rates have led to a 27-percent decline in the volume of balsam fir and a 14-percent decline in the volume of paper birch.

- The majority of sawtimber is in lower valued tree grade 3 for both hardwoods (52 percent) and softwoods (77 percent).

- Just over half (53 percent) of the forest land in Minnesota is fully stocked or overstocked compared to 57 percent in Wisconsin and 62 percent in Michigan.

- The average annual mortality for Minnesota over 1990 to 2002 was 272 million cubic feet. This is equal to 1.8 percent of the total growing-stock volume in 2003—a rate significantly higher than the 1.2 percent reported in 1977 and the 1.3 percent reported in 1990.

- Mortality from larch beetles, chestnut borers, spruce beetles, and oak wilt continue to affect Minnesota's forests, but adverse weather continues to cause the most significant damage.

- Eastern spruce budworm, forest tent caterpillar, jack pine budworm, introduced larch casebearer, and other defoliating agents have been active, sometimes on some of the same land at the same time. Many trees that are repeatedly defoliated sustain measurable growth loss, which in turn, may lead to mortality.

- European gypsy moth egg masses were discovered in several places including one location just 1 mile from the Boundary Waters Canoe Area Wilderness (BWCAW). It is only a matter of time before this pest becomes permanently established in Minnesota.

- The emerald ash borer has been found in Michigan, Indiana, and Ohio and may eventually threaten Minnesota's ash trees.

- A small sub-sample of 38 plots was measured to assess the occurrence of invasive species. Introduced or invasive plant species were found on 45 percent of these vegetative diversity plots. These invasive species could displace native species, harming native ecosystems.

- The effects of the BWCAW blowdown of July 4, 1999, were still being seen in northeastern Minnesota in higher amounts of large down woody fuels when compared to Michigan and Wisconsin.

- The area of interior forest (continuous forest canopy for surrounding 6 acres) declined between 1992 and 2001, partly because of housing construction in nonmetropolitan counties.

- The average private landholding size decreased from 39 acres in 1982 to 31 acres in 2003.

Decreasing area of forest land. The area of forest land is estimated to have decreased by 4 percent between 1990 and 2003. And projections from the national timber assessment indicate the area of timberland may decrease by 9 percent over the next 50 years.

Increasing fragmentation and parcelization. Forest fragmentation occurs when a contiguous forest area is divided into smaller blocks—usually through the construction of roads and housing, clearing for agriculture, or other human development. Parcelization is the process by which large holdings by one owner are broken up into smaller holdings by multiple owners.

Fragmentation and parcelization have adverse effects on the forest including the loss of biodiversity, increased populations of invasive and nonnative tree species, and changes in biotic and abiotic environments. They may also lead to changing landowner objectives and decreased or more costly natural resources as in the case of timber management.

Introduction of invasive species may have significant negative effects on Minnesota's forests. The European gypsy moth and the emerald ash borer are just two of the many species that threaten midwestern forests.

The Features, Health, and Products of Minnesota's Forests

To Be Precise...A Beginners Guide to Forest Inventory

Every thing is vague to a degree you do not realize till you have tried to make it precise.
—Bertrand Russell (1872-1970)

What is a Tree?

We all know a tree when we see one. And we can agree on some common tree attributes. Trees are perennial woody plants having central stems and distinct crowns. In general, we in FIA define a tree as any perennial woody plant species that can attain a height of 15 feet at maturity. In Minnesota, the problem is in deciding which species should be classified as shrubs and which should be classified as trees. A complete list of the tree species measured during this inventory can be found in Part B, the companion to this document.

What is a Forest?

We all know what a forest is but where does the forest stop and the prairie begin? It is an important question. The gross area of forest land or rangeland often determines the allocation of funding for certain State and Federal programs. Forest managers want more land classified as forest land; range managers want more land classified as prairie. Somewhere you have to draw the line.

FIA defines forest land as land at least 10 percent stocked by trees of any size or formerly having had such tree cover and not currently developed for nonforest use. The area with trees must be at least 1 acre in size, and roadside, streamside, and shelterbelt strips must be at least 120 feet wide to qualify as forest land.

What is the Difference Among Timberland, Reserved Forest Land and Other Forest Land?

From an FIA perspective, there are three types of forest land: timberland, reserved forest land, and other forest land. In Minnesota, 91 percent of the forest land is timberland, 6 percent is reserved forest land, and 3 percent is other forest land.

Most of the reserved forest land in Minnesota is in the Boundary Waters Canoe Area Wilderness and Voyagers National Park, land withdrawn from timber utilization through legislation or administrative regulation. The other forest land in Minnesota is typically found on low-lying sites with poor soils where the forest is incapable of producing 20 cubic feet/acre/year at its peak. Timberland is forest land that is not reserved and meets minimum productivity requirements.

In prior inventories we measured trees only on timberland plots and could not report volume on all forest land. With the implementation of the new annual inventory system in 1999, we can now report volume on all forest land, not just on timberland. As these annual plots are remeasured in the years ahead, we will also be able to report growth, removals, and mortality on all forest land. In this report, trend reporting is necessarily limited to timberland except for the area of forest land where individual tree measurements are not required.

Measure what is measurable, and make measurable what is not so.

-- Galileo Galilei (1564-1642)

How Many Trees are There in Minnesota?

There are approximately 2.2 billion trees on Minnesota's forest land (give or take a few million) that are at least 5 inches in diameter as measured at 4.5 feet above the ground. We do not know the exact number because we measured only about 1 out of every 18 thousand trees[1]. In all, 106,710 trees were sampled on 4,486 forested plots. For information on sampling errors, see Part B.

How Do We Estimate a Tree's Volume?

Forest inventory has typically expressed volumes in cubic feet. In Minnesota, wood is more commonly measured in cords (a stack of wood 8 feet long, 4 feet wide, and 4 feet high). A cord of wood has approximately 79 cubic feet of solid wood and 49 cubic feet of bark and air.

Volume can be precisely determined by immersing the tree in a pool of water and measuring the amount of water displaced. Less precise, but much cheaper, was the method used by the North Central Research Station. In this method, several hundred cut trees were measured taking detailed diameter measurements along their lengths to accurately determine their volumes (Hahn 1984). Regression lines were then fit to this data by species group. Using these regression equations, we can produce individual tree volume estimates based on species, diameter, and tree site index.

The same method was used to determine sawtimber volumes. FIA reports sawtimber volumes in International one-fourth-inch board foot scale. Conversion factors for converting to Scribner board foot scale are also available (Smith 1991).

How Much Does a Tree Weigh? Eureka!

Building on the work of the Greek mathematician Archimedes (circa 287 B.C.-212 B.C.), the Forest Products Laboratory of the USDA Forest Service developed specific gravity estimates for a number of tree species (USDA FPL 1999). These specific gravities were then applied to tree volume estimates to estimate merchantable tree biomass (the weight of the bole). It gets a little more complicated when we want to determine all-live biomass. We have to add in the stump (Raile 1982) and the limbs and bark (Hahn 1984). We do not currently report the biomass in roots or foliage.

Forest inventory can report biomass as either green weight or ovendry weight. Green weight is the weight of a freshly cut tree. Ovendry weight is the weight of a tree with zero percent moisture content. On average, one ton of ovendry biomass is equal to 1.9 tons of green biomass.

---

[1] *During the 2003 inventory of Minnesota (from 1999 to 2003), we measured four 1/24th acre subplots (for a total area of 1/6th acre) for approximately every 3,000 acres of forest land.*

13

How Do We Compare Data from Different Inventories?

Data from new inventories are often compared with data from earlier inventories to determine trends in forest resources. However, for comparisons to be valid, procedures used in the two inventories must be similar. As a result of FIA's ongoing efforts to improve the efficiency and reliability of the inventory, several changes in procedures and definitions have occurred since the last Minnesota inventory in 1990. While these changes will have little effect on statewide estimates of forest area, timber volume, and tree biomass, they may have significant effects on plot classification variables such as forest type and stand-size class. Some of these changes make it inappropriate to directly compare 2003 data tables with those published for 1990.

The biggest change between inventories was the change in plot design. For consistency's sake, a new national plot design was implemented by all five regional FIA units in 1999. The old North Central plot design used in the 1990 Minnesota inventory consisted of variable-radius subplots. The new national plot design used in the 2003 inventory used fixed-radius subplots. Both designs have their strong points, but they often produce different classifications for individual plot characteristics.

The 1990 inventory also used modeled plots—plots measured in 1977 and projected forward using the STEMS (Belcher et al. 1982) growth model. This was done to save money by reducing the number of undisturbed plots that were sent to the field for remeasurement, where disturbance was determined by examining aerial photographs of the plots. The idea was that parameters for the STEMS growth model could be fine-tuned using the measured undisturbed plots and then applied to the remaining unmeasured undisturbed plots. Unfortunately, the use of modeled plots appears to have overestimated the 1990 all-live volume on timberland by approximately 6 percent. Therefore, in this paper, when comparisons are made with the 1990 inventory, only field measured plots are used.

In a progressive country, change is constant; … change … is inevitable

Benjamin Disraeli (1804-1881)

A Word of Caution on Suitability and Availability…

FIA does not attempt to identify which lands are suitable or available for timber harvesting—especially since suitability and availability are subject to changing laws and ownership objectives. Just because land is classified as timberland does not necessarily mean it is suitable or available for timber production. There are several reasons why timberland may not be available for timber production.

> *Laws and regulations:* Laws protect historic and cultural sites as well as endangered species. According to the Minnesota Forest Resources Council (MFRC 2005) "…private forest landowners do not need a permit to cut trees, but in certain instances do need a permit to cross a stream with logging equipment. They also may have to follow restrictions on timber harvesting imposed by various local units of government. For instance, counties have shore-land ordinances that public and private landowners must follow … An array of other laws, rules and agency procedures govern public forest land management."

Voluntary guidelines: As a result of the Minnesota Sustainable Forest Resource Act of 1995 and 1999, the MFRC developed a set of voluntary guidelines to help protect historic and cultural resources, riparian areas, soil productivity, visual quality, water quality, wetlands, and wildlife habitat.

Ownership objectives: In response to the National Woodland Landowner Survey conducted by FIA, 5.8 percent of private landowners owning 19.4 percent of the private forest land in Minnesota stated they intended to harvest saw logs or pulpwood within the next 5 years. Many landowners chose not to harvest out of concern over esthetic or visual impacts on their property (Carpenter et al. 1986) while others felt harvesting would have a detrimental effect on hunting. Still other landowners felt that physical characteristics of the resource, such as low volume, immature timber, poor quality, or too small an area, would deter them from harvesting.

The bottom line is that forest inventory data alone are inadequate for determining the area of forest land available for timber production. Several other factors need to be considered when estimating the timber base including laws and regulations, voluntary guidelines, and ownership objectives, and these in turn may change with time

Where are Minnesota's Forests?

Ecoregion Provinces of Minnesota

Minnesota is at the confluence of three ecoprovinces (Bailey 1976): the Laurentian Mixed Forest Province in the northeastern part of the State, the Eastern Broadleaf Forest Province through the center, and the Prairie Parkland Province in the west (fig. 2.1). Boundaries of these provinces are largely determined by geology and climate.

Figure 2.1. Bailey's ecoregion provinces of Minnesota.

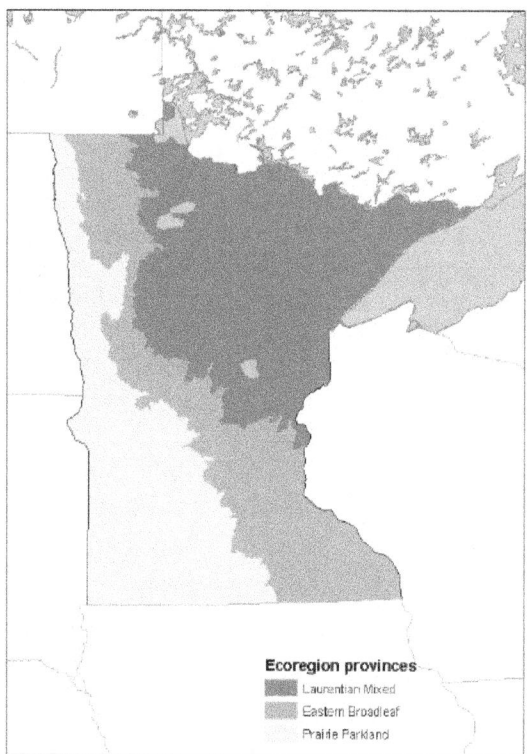

Ecoregion provinces
Laurentian Mixed
Eastern Broadleaf
Prairie Parkland

The Laurentian province lies in the transition zone between the Canadian boreal forests to the north and the broadleaf deciduous forests to the south and west. Much of the province consists of mixed stands of coniferous and deciduous species. Coniferous species dominate in habitats with poor soils while deciduous species dominate in favorable habitats with good soils.

Mixed stands have several species of conifers, mainly northern white-cedar. Eastern redcedar is found in the southeast. Pine trees are often the pioneer woody species that flourish in burned-over areas or on abandoned arable land. Because pines grow more rapidly than deciduous species in poor soils, they quickly form a forest canopy. However, where deciduous undergrowth is dense, conifers have trouble regenerating and remain successful only where fire recurs.

The Broadleaf province is dominated by deciduous forests. The northern reaches of the province are dominated by maple/basswood giving way to drought-resistant oak/hickory in the south. The oak/hickory forest is medium-tall to tall, becoming savanna-like and gradually turning into prairie in the western reaches.

The Prairie province is characterized by intermingled prairie, groves, and strips of deciduous trees. The alternation of forest and prairie in the western part of the province results chiefly from local soil conditions and slope exposure; trees are commonly found near streams and on north-facing slopes.

The upland forest in this province is dominated by oak and hickory. On floodplains and moist hillsides, the deciduous forest is richer. In the western part of the province, it includes eastern cottonwood, black willow, and American elm.

The area of forest land is currently concentrated in the Laurentian province (fig. 2.2) where several counties are more than 70 percent forested. Lesser amounts of forest land occur in the Broadleaf province and the least occurs in the drier Prairie province.

Overall, Minnesota is nearly 32 percent forest land. It ranks 14th among the 50 States in land area, 19th in forest land area, and 12th in timberland area.

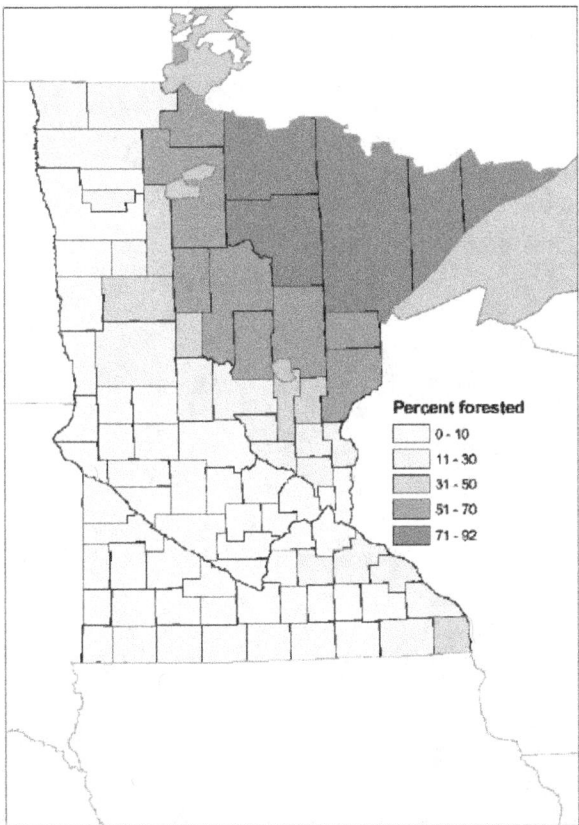

Figure 2.2. Percentage of land forested by county, Minnesota, 2003.

Distribution of Forest Land by Forest Type

Information from forest inventory plots was combined with ancillary data (see Data Sources and Techniques section) to produce a forest type map where aspen, pine, and spruce/fir types predominate in the north and the oak and elm/ash/cottonwood types predominate in the south (fig. 2.3).

Figure 2.3. Forest types of Minnesota, 2003.

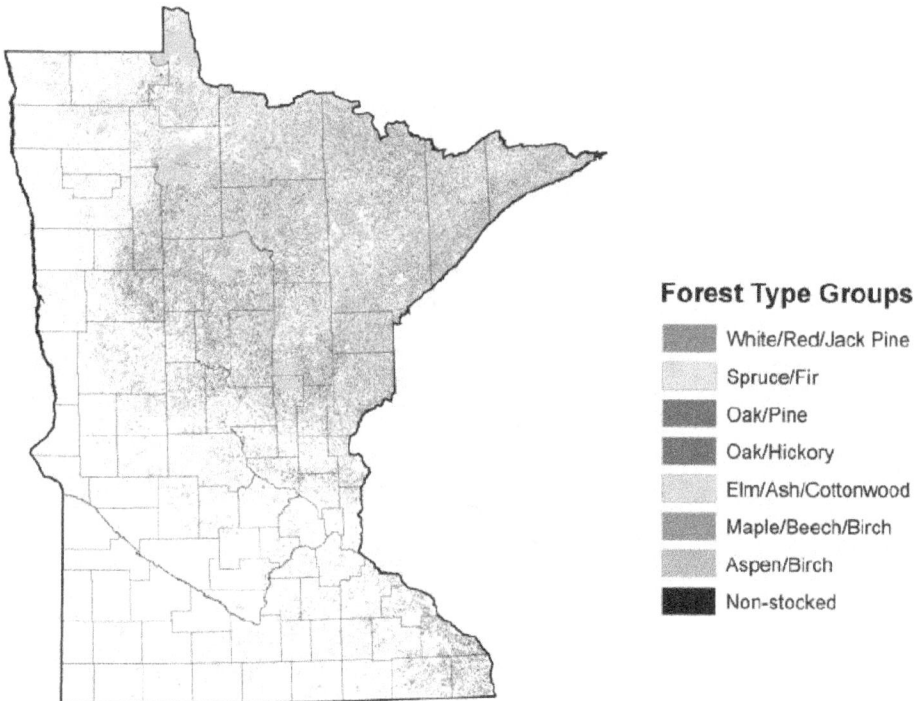

Forest Type Groups

- White/Red/Jack Pine
- Spruce/Fir
- Oak/Pine
- Oak/Hickory
- Elm/Ash/Cottonwood
- Maple/Beech/Birch
- Aspen/Birch
- Non-stocked

The top 12 forest types in Minnesota account for 95 percent of the forest land (fig. 2.4). Aspen is the largest forest type in Minnesota, accounting for 31 percent of Minnesota's forest land (5.1 million acres), followed by the northern hardwood type at 12 percent and the black spruce type at 10 percent.

Figure 2.4. Percentage of forest land area by forest type, Minnesota 2003.

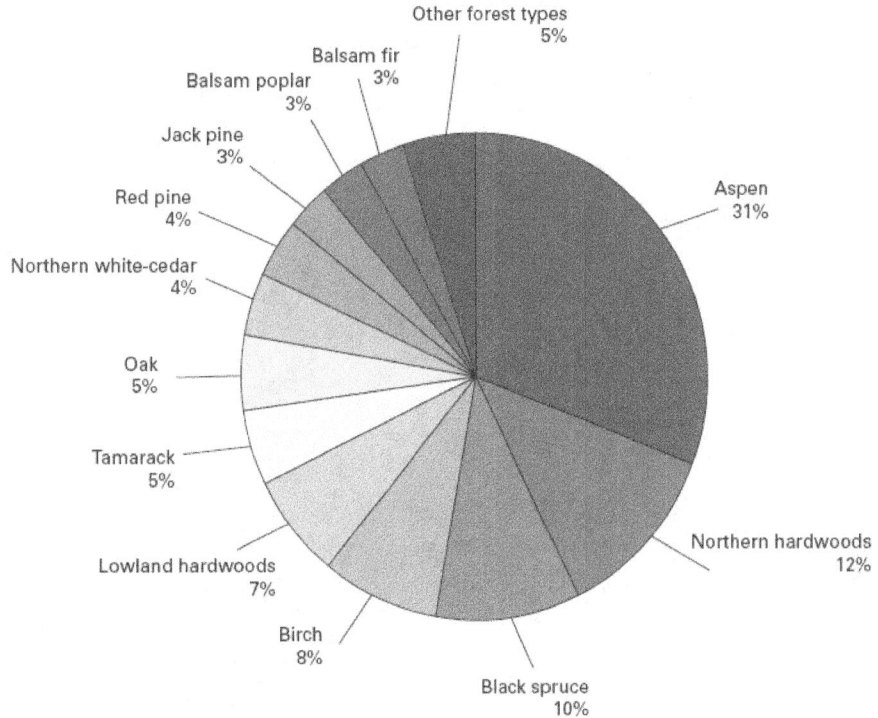

Distribution of Forest Land by Ownership

More than half of the forest land in Minnesota is publicly owned (fig. 2.5, 2.6). The State of Minnesota owns 24 percent; county and local governments own 16 percent; and the Federal government administers 17 percent of Minnesota's forest land. Most of the Federal lands are concentrated in the northern part of the State in Voyageurs National Park, the Chippewa National Forest, the Superior National Forest, and the Boundary Waters Canoe Area Wilderness (BWCAW) (fig. 2.7).

The remaining 43 percent of Minnesota's forest land is privately owned. Only 7 percent of Minnesota's forest land is owned by forest industry and corporations compared to 8.5 percent in Wisconsin and 13.5 percent in Michigan. More than four-fifths of forest industry and corporate lands are located in just four counties (Itasca, Koochiching, Lake, and St. Louis). Even in these four counties, forest industry and corporations own only 13 percent of the forest land.

Nonindustrial private forest landowners hold the remaining 36 percent of the forest land in Minnesota.

Figure 2.5. Forest land by ownership or administering governmental unit, Minnesota, 2003.

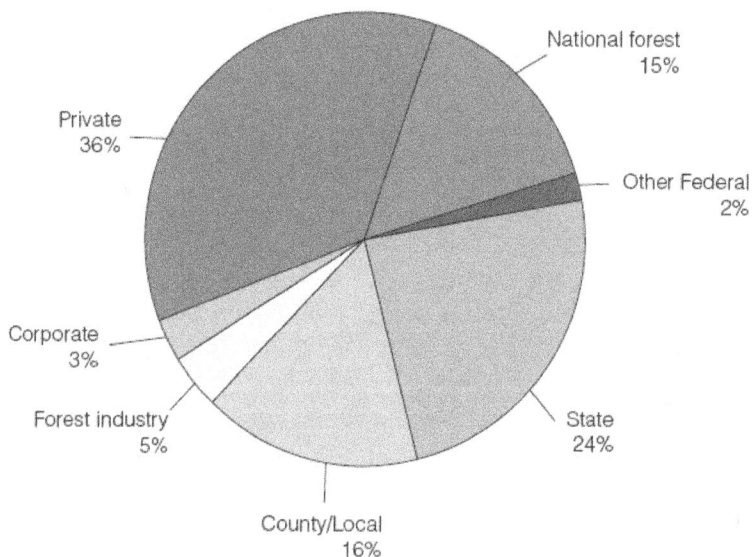

Figure 2.6. Public and private forest land ownership, Minnesota, 2003.

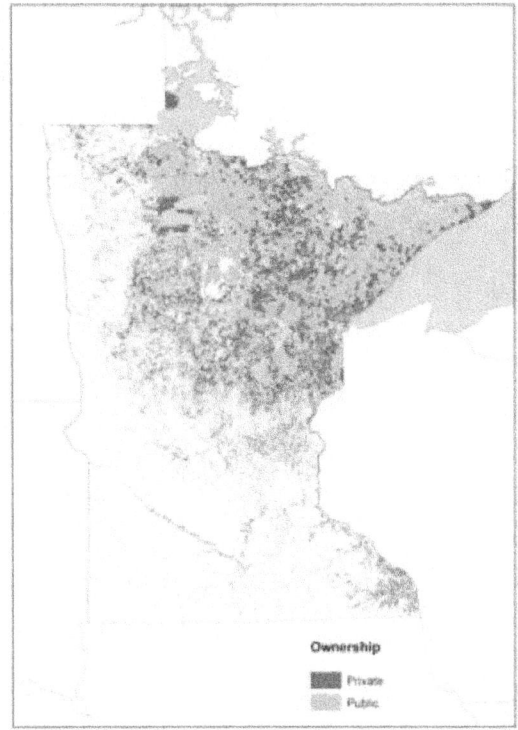

Figure 2.7. Federally administered forest lands of Minnesota, 2003.

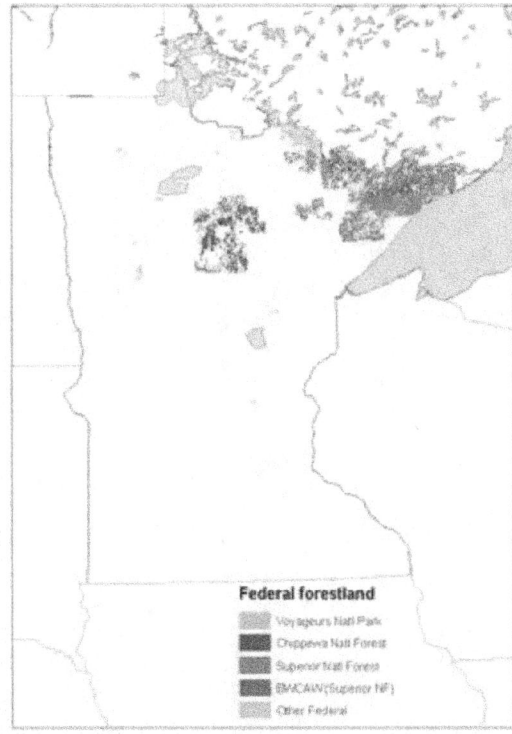

Forest Features

Forest Area

Background:

Area estimates, the most basic of all forest inventory estimates, are essential in assessing the status and trends of Minnesota's forest ecosystems. Fluctuations in the forest land base may indicate land use trends and changing forest health conditions.

What We Found:

Minnesota's forest land area is currently estimated at 16.2 million acres or roughly 32 percent of the land area of the State (fig. 3.1).

The presettlement area of forest land was estimated to be 31.5 million acres (Marschner 1930). The largest decline in the area of forest land occurred before the first forest inventory was conducted in the mid-1930s, and was due to lumbering followed by homesteading and land clearing (Zon 1935). This decline continued through the first four inventories of Minnesota. Between 1977 and 1990, a small increase (0.7 percent) in the area of forest land was recorded. Since 1990 the area of forest land has declined (in figure 3.1 the decline from 1990 to 2003 is 2.6 percent although the real decline is closer to 4 percent when adjusted for definitional changes between surveys—for an explanation of these definitional changes, see the section on land use change under Forest Change Issues).

Changes in the area of forest land appear to vary regionally. Ninety percent of Minnesota's forest land lies above the 46th parallel, which runs through the town of Hinckley (fig. 3.2). Since 1977 there has been a 4-percent decline in the area of forest land above this line, from 15.1 million acres in 1977 to 14.6 million in 2003. Below this line, the area of forest land has increased by about 10 percent from 1.5 million to 1.6 million acres.

In 1977 there were an estimated 13.7 million acres of timberland in Minnesota. The estimate of timberland increased to 14.7 million acres by 1990 and slightly increased to 14.8 million acres by 2003, although this latest increase was due in part to changing estimates of site productivity.

What This Means:

The area and extent of Minnesota's forests have been decreasing since the first forest inventory in 1935. Much of the losses to forest area have been offset by the reversion of marginal farmland and pasture land to forest. The slight increase in forest land area from 1977 to 1990 was due in part to the Federal government's Conservation Reserve Program. Under this program, erosion-prone cropland was removed from crop production and often reverted to forest land. The loss of forest land between 1990 and 2003 was due to diversion to marshland, urban uses, pasture, farmland, and rights-of-way.

Increases in the area of timberland between 1977 and 2003 were due in part to changing estimates of site productivity. The area of other forest land declined substantially from 1.9 million acres in 1977 to 840 thousand acres in 1990 to 528 thousand acres in 2003. Nearly half of the other forest land lost was converted to nonforest land, and the other half was converted to timberland. Since 1977 nearly 700 thousand acres once classified as other forest land have been reclassified as timberland.

Figure 3.1. Area of forest land in Minnesota by inventory year.[2]

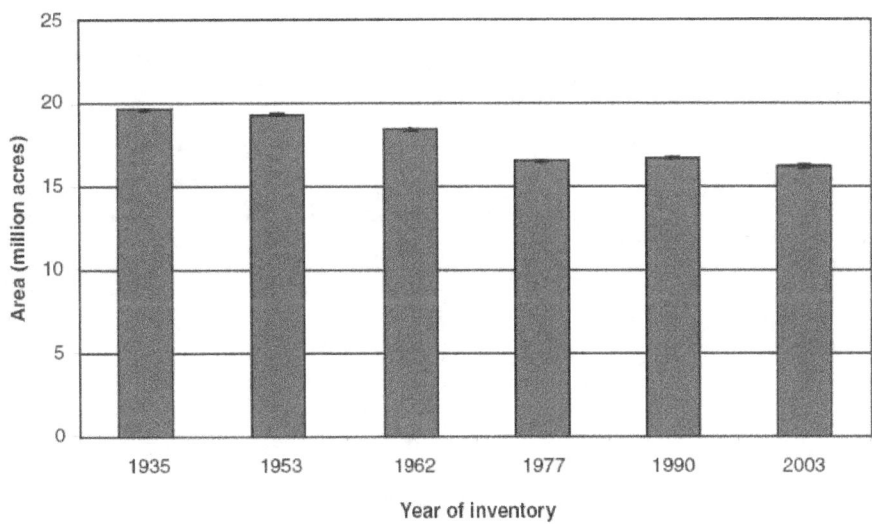

Figure 3.2. Forest area from National Land Cover Dataset.

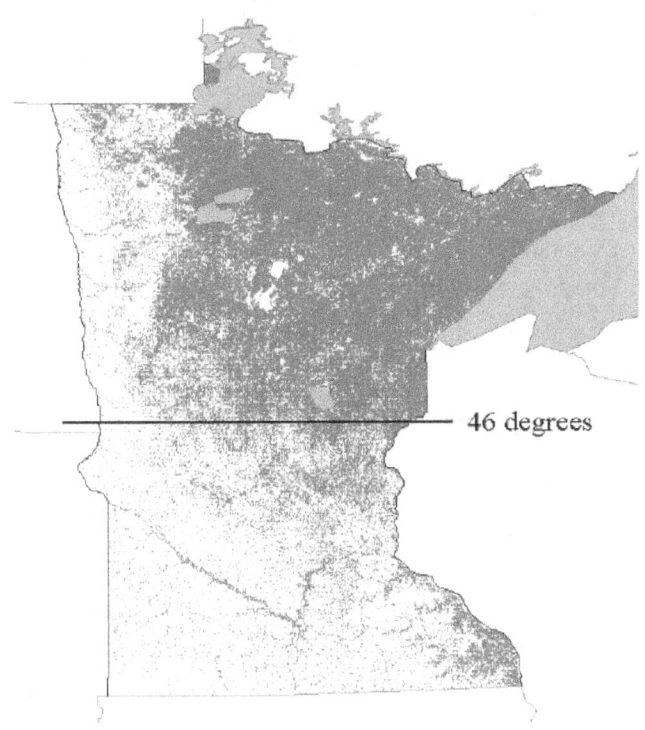

46 degrees

_____

[2] The error bars atop each bar in figure 3.1 provides a measure of reliability of this figure. In 2003 there was a two out of three chance that if a 100-percent inventory had been taken, using the same methods, the result would have been within the limits indicated by the error bar—16,230.3 thousand acres plus or minus 102.3 thousand acres.

Number of Trees

Background:

An estimate of the number of trees in a forest is useful only when combined with information about the diameters of the trees. Young forests have many more trees per acre than older forests, but older forests have much more biomass than younger forests. The number of trees and their diameter distributions are what's important.

What We Found:

There are currently an estimated 12 billion trees on forest land in Minnesota. More than 81 percent of these trees are saplings (trees that are from 1 to 5 inches in diameter), 15 percent are poletimber-size trees (5 to 9 inches for softwoods and 5 to 11 inches for hardwoods), and 4 percent are sawtimber-size trees. Nearly two-thirds of the trees in Minnesota are hardwoods and the rest are softwoods. Quaking aspen alone accounts for more than 30 percent of the total number of trees in Minnesota.

The total number of trees in Minnesota increased from 1977 to 2003. The number of sapling and sawtimber trees increased, and the number of poletimber trees decreased (fig. 3.3).

There were large increases in the number of poletimber-size red pine, sugar maple, black ash, black spruce, American basswood, bur oak, and northern white-cedar between 1977 and 2003. There were large decreases in the number of northern red oak, quaking aspen, paper birch, and balsam fir. Surprisingly, the number of saplings increased over the period for the 12 most common tree species. This was especially true for quaking aspen, which increased from 1.2 billion saplings in 1977 to 3.0 billion saplings in 2003. Half of the increase in the number of saplings was due to just the increase in aspen.

Between 1977 and 2003, the number of all-live aspen trees between 5 and 11 inches in diameter decreased significantly (fig. 3.4). There was a significant increase in the number of aspen trees from 1 to 5 inches in diameter. The all-live volume of aspen actually decreased from 3.9 billion cubic feet in 1977 to 3.5 billion cubic feet in 2003. Fortunately, a large amount of recruitment is coming in the smaller diameter classes and the volume of aspen will increase significantly as these saplings grow into the larger diameter classes.

What This Means:

Aspen has not always been a dominant species in the State and, in fact, was a minor component of the forest before the logging boom in the late 1800s to the early 1900s (Leatherberry et al. 1995). Aspen is an opportunistic, short-lived pioneer species that moved in to claim many sites after logging. Before the 1970s, quaking aspen was viewed as a "weed" tree. Today, aspen is of great economic importance in the State, and a greater percentage of its volume is harvested than any other species in Minnesota (3.3 percent per year). Fortunately, there is no problem regenerating aspen. Once aspen is harvested, it quickly repopulates the area through root sprouting.

Figure 3.3. Number of all-live trees by size class, Minnesota, 1977, 1990, 2003.

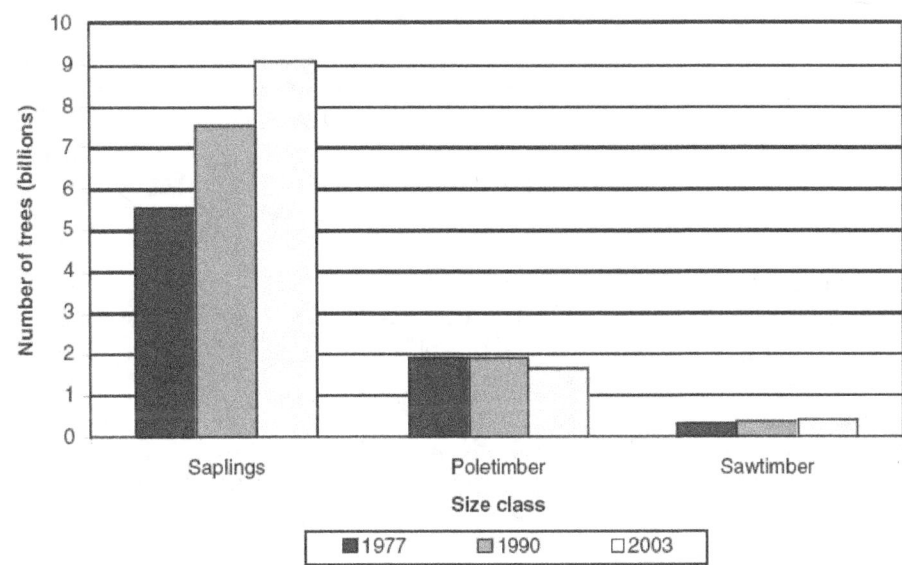

Figure 3.4. Number of all-live aspen trees by diameter class, Minnesota, 1977, 1990, 2003.

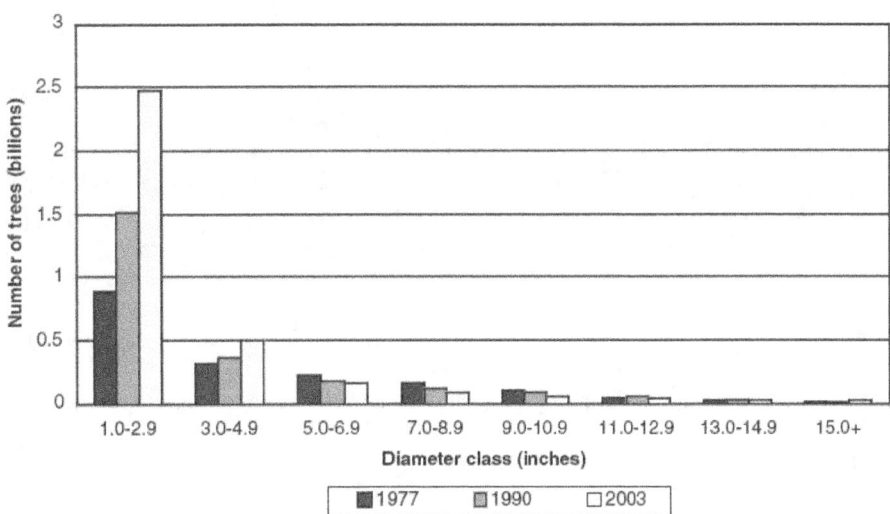

Tree Biomass

Background:

Biomass estimates are increasing in importance for analyses of carbon sequestration, wood fiber availability for fuel, and other issues. Traditionally timber harvests have been measured in board feet or cubic feet. Increasingly they are measured in green tons or dry tons. In Minnesota, the ratio of green tons to dry tons is approximately 1.9 to 1.0.

What We Found:

Biomass, measured as all-live aboveground tree biomass on forest land, was estimated at 465 million dry tons in 2003 (an average of 28.7 dry tons per acre of forest land). The distribution of forest biomass per acre of land is presented in figure 3.5.

The average dry weight of a tree (includes stump, bole, and limbs but excludes foliage and roots) increases dramatically with increasing tree diameter (table 3.1). The average tree in the 7.0- to 8.9-inch diameter class, for example, weighs slightly more than twice the average tree in the 5.0- to 6.9-inch class.

In 2003, 78 percent of the total biomass was in growing-stock trees, 14 percent was in trees less than 5 inches d.b.h., and 8 percent was in non-growing-stock trees (fig. 3.6). Nearly three-quarters of the total biomass was composed of hardwood species. Although total biomass was almost evenly split on private (221 million dry tons) and public (244 million dry tons) forest lands, softwoods made up 36 percent of the total biomass on public lands, but only 15 percent on private lands.

The total all-live dry biomass on timberland in 1977 was 409 million tons. By 2003 this had increased by 5.6 percent to 432 million tons. This increase was due to the increasing size of the trees in Minnesota. In 1977 half of the all-live tree biomass on timberland was in trees less than 8.8 inches d.b.h.; by 2003 the midpoint was 9.9 inches (fig 3.7). Biomass increased in sawtimber and sapling trees and decreased in poletimber trees.

What This Means:

Minnesota is continuing to gain biomass due to the continued maturation of the State's forests even while it is losing forest area. The live tree biomass of Minnesota's forests represents only one source of forest ecosystem carbon. Other substantial pools of carbon are found in forest soils, standing dead trees, down dead trees, roots, and nontree vegetation.

Figure 3.5. Average all-live tree biomass in tons per acre of forest land, Minnesota, 2003.

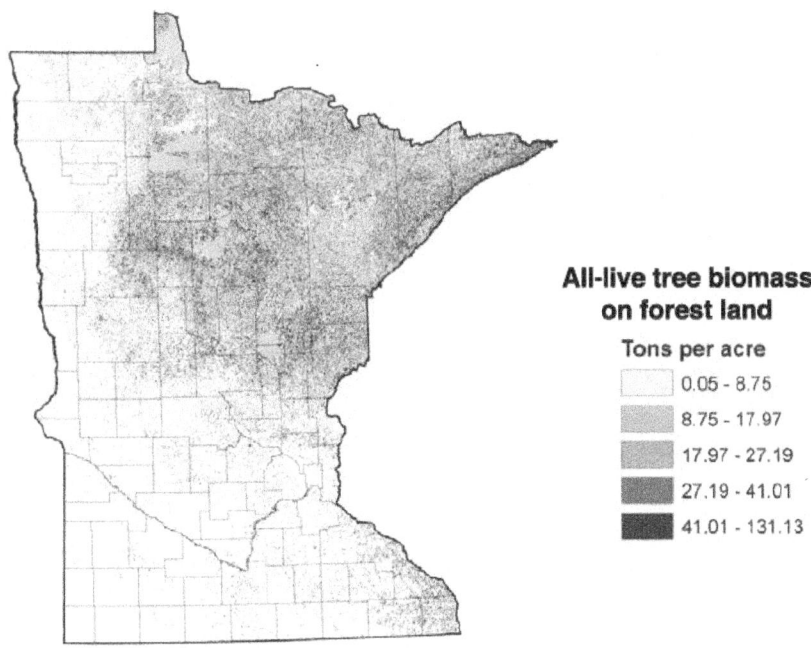

All-live tree biomass on forest land

Tons per acre

	0.05 - 8.75
	8.75 - 17.97
	17.97 - 27.19
	27.19 - 41.01
	41.01 - 131.13

Table 3.1. Average dry tree biomass in pounds by diameter class (inches) and softwood/hardwood category

Diameter class	Softwoods	Hardwoods
1.0-2.9	6	6
3.0-4.9	34	41
5.0-6.9	101	134
7.0-8.9	204	286
9.0-10.9	341	489
11.0-12.9	515	748
13.0-14.9	729	1,062
15.0-16.9	1,024	1,448
17.0-18.9	1,379	1,933
19.0-20.9	1,853	2,443
21.0-28.9	2,780	3,708
29.0+	5,642	7,386

Figure 3.6. Live tree biomass by tree component, Minnesota, 2003.

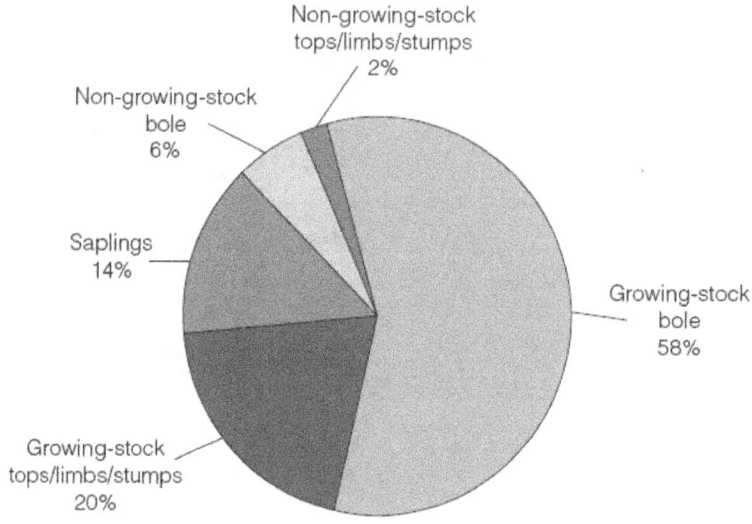

Figure 3.7. All-live dry biomass on timberland by major species group and 2-inch diameter classes, Minnesota, 1977, 2003.

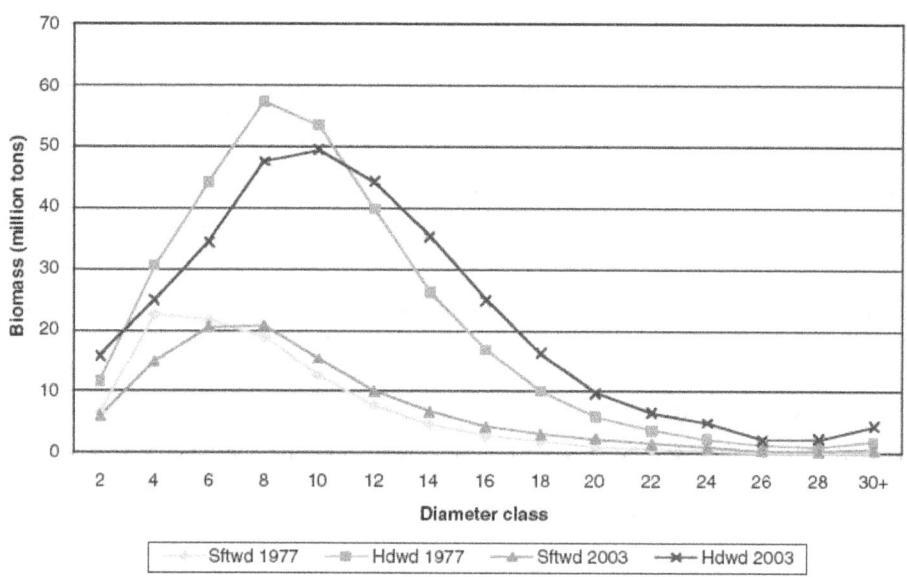

Volume and Species Composition

Background:

Current volumes can be compared to rates of harvest to aid in determining the sustainability of current and projected future harvest levels. Because certain species are more economically desirable than other species, it is important to view volume information on a species by species basis.

What We Found:

The volume of growing-stock trees on timberland in Minnesota increased from 12.3 billion cubic feet in 1977 to 14.2 billion cubic feet[3] in 1990 to 15.3 billion in 2003. Reporting growing-stock volume on timberland is important for historical purposes because growth, mortality, and removals figures are available only for growing stock on timberland. The volume of all-live trees on timberland increased from 14.3 billion cubic feet in 1977 to 16.3 billion in 2003.

The majority of softwoods are located in north-central and northeastern Minnesota (fig. 3.8).

Ninety-eight percent of all-live tree volume on forest land comes from just 24 of the 66 species measured during the 2003 inventory. Leading the list is quaking aspen at 21 percent, followed by paper birch (8 percent), northern white-cedar (6 percent), and black spruce (5 percent).

Figure 3.9 shows the change in growing-stock volume on timberland by species for the 12 species that had the largest volume in 2003 (73 percent of the total). Between 1977 and 2003, the big winners included tamarack, which increased in volume by 117 percent, sugar maple (95 percent), red pine (91 percent), bur oak (84 percent), and northern white-cedar (77 percent). The losers included balsam fir with a 27-percent decline and paper birch (14 percent).

The aspen resource is concentrated in northeastern Minnesota (fig. 3.10). The decrease in growing-stock volume of aspen from 1990 to 2003 was due primarily to high levels of removals. Growing-stock volume on timberland decreased by 8 percent, from 3.6 billion cubic feet in 1990 to 3.3 billion cubic feet in 2003.

All-live volume per acre on timberland increased from 1,050 cubic feet/acre in 1977 to 1,082 cubic feet/ace in 1990 to 1,107 cubic feet/acre in 2003.

What This Means:

Aspen volumes are still near historically high levels although there has been a moderate decline as a result of current demand. The supply of aspen may increase in the near term as a tremendous number of sapling-size stands move into merchantable size. Demand for aspen may increase as new bioenergy plants go on line.

Volumes of most other species have increased except for balsam fir and paper birch (which had very high rates of mortality). Removals rates for these species are significantly lower than those for aspen.

---

[3] The 1990 growing-stock volume was recalculated using only field measured plots. Modeled plot information was excluded because it overestimated volumes.

Figure 3.8. Percentage of all-live volume in softwood species, Minnesota, 2003.

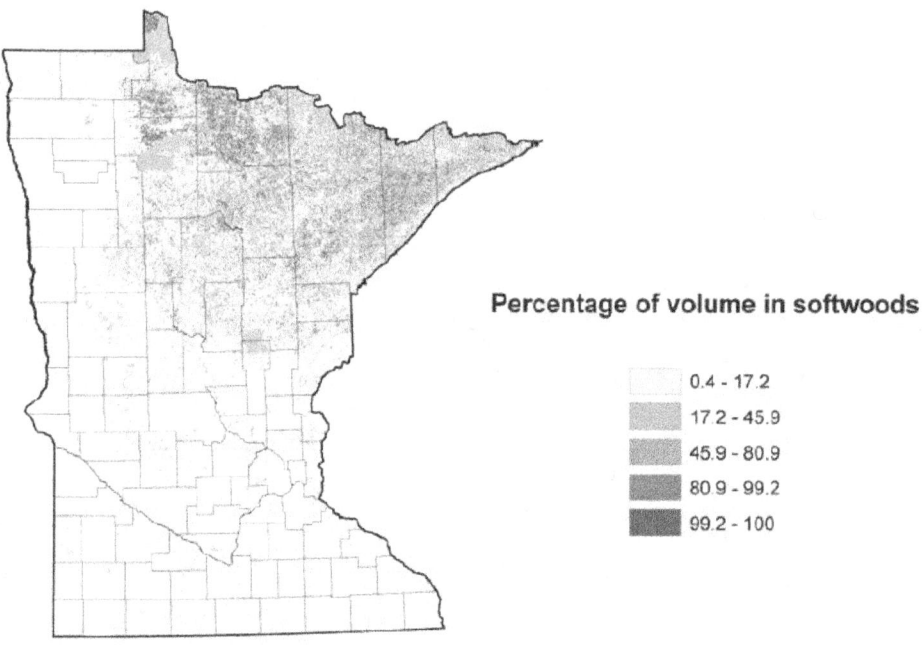

Percentage of volume in softwoods

0.4 - 17.2
17.2 - 45.9
45.9 - 80.9
80.9 - 99.2
99.2 - 100

Figure 3.9. Growing-stock volume by species on timberland, Minnesota, 1977, 1990, 2003.

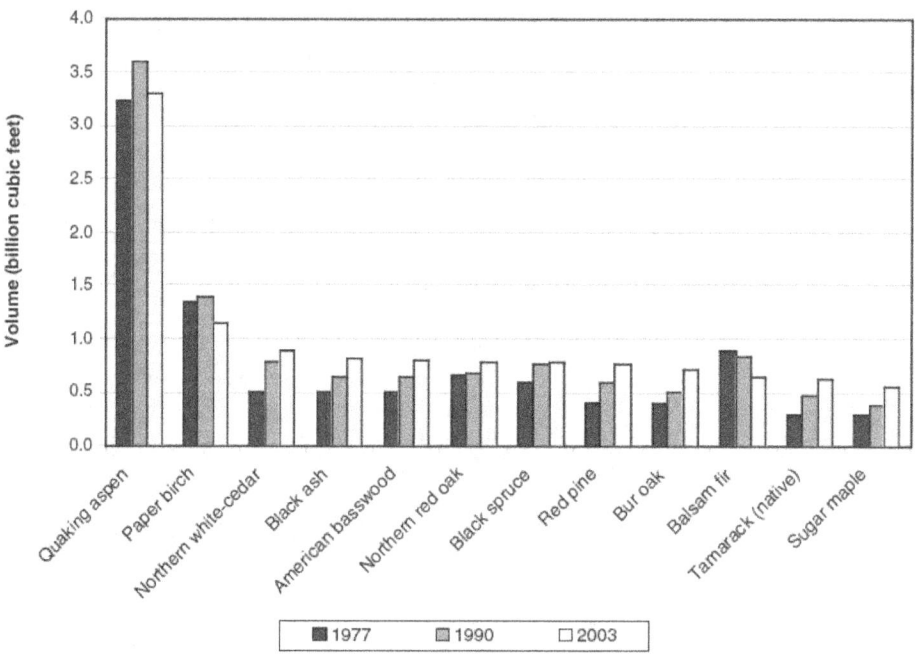

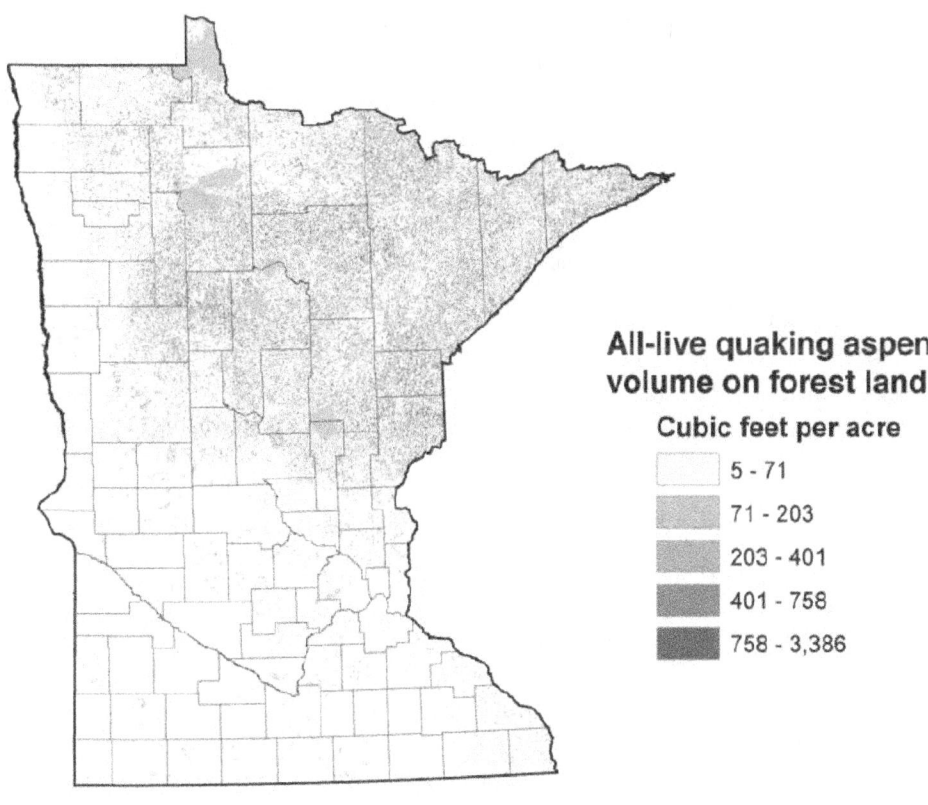

Figure 3.10. All-live tree volume of quaking aspen on forest land, Minnesota, 2003.

All-live quaking aspen volume on forest land

Cubic feet per acre

5 - 71
71 - 203
203 - 401
401 - 758
758 - 3,386

Sawtimber Volume and Quality

Background:

A board foot is a unit of measure 1 inch by 1 inch by 12 inches. Tree grade is based on tree diameter and the presence or absence of knots, decay, or curvature of the bole. The value of sawtimber varies greatly by species and tree grade. The highest quality trees are graded 1; the lowest quality trees are graded 4.

Softwood sawtimber is primarily valued for dimensional lumber while hardwood sawtimber is valued for use in flooring and furniture. Softwoods must be at least 9 inches in diameter to qualify as sawtimber-size tree, hardwoods must be at least 11 inches in diameter.

What We Found:

In 2003, 42.2 billion board feet of sawtimber were on Minnesota's forest land. Approximately 8 percent of the sawtimber volume was found on reserved and unproductive forest land. Of the 38.7 billion board feet of sawtimber on timberland, nearly two-thirds were in hardwoods (25.1 billion board feet) and the rest were in softwoods (13.6 billion board feet).

The volume of sawtimber increased steadily between inventories, from 23.7 billion board feet in 1977 to 30.7 in 1990 and 38.7 in 2003 (fig. 3.11).

Of the 66 species measured on FIA plots during the 2003 inventory, 44 had trees that had attained sawtimber size. More than three-quarters of the sawtimber volume was found in just 12 species (fig. 3.12). The volume in each of these species has been increasing since 1977 with the notable exceptions of quaking aspen, jack pine, and balsam fir.

The majority of sawtimber is in tree grade 3 for both hardwoods (52 percent) and softwoods (77 percent) (fig. 3.13). Tree grade 2 represents 34 percent of total hardwood volume and 14 percent of softwood volume. The most valuable lumber is in grade 1, which constitutes just 9 percent and 7 percent of hardwood and softwood volumes, respectively.

What This Means:

The volume and quality of sawtimber in the State are increasing except for pioneer species like quaking aspen and jack pine and species that have had high rates of mortality such as balsam fir, American elm, and butternut. The volume of sawtimber per acre of timberland increased by 50 percent between 1977 and 2003. Increases in sawtimber volume occurred on all ownerships. Sawtimber volumes per acre are especially high on Federal land where the average board foot volume per acre of timberland increased from 2,275 in 1977 to 3,193 in 2003. Sawtimber volume per acre also increased for forests administered by State and local governments (from 1,432 to 2,149) and on privately owned land (from 1,826 to 2,871).

Figure 3.11. Sawtimber volume on timberland by hardwoods and softwoods and inventory year, Minnesota.

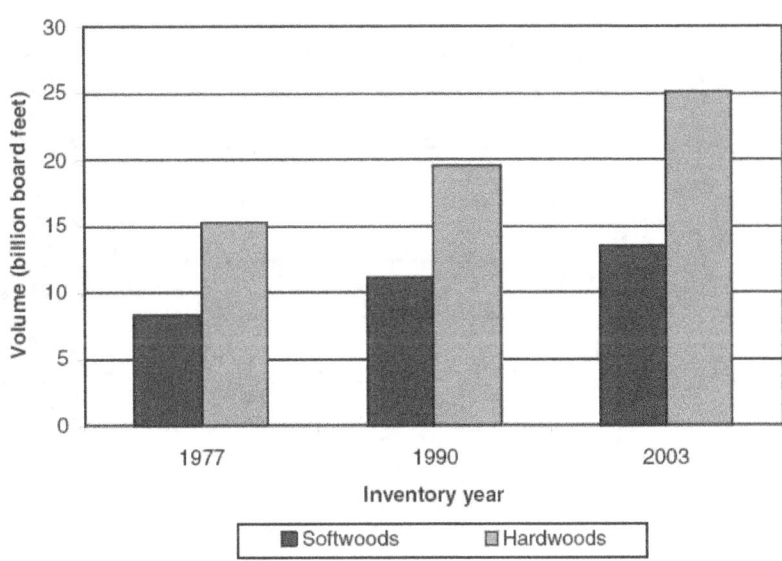

Figure 3.12. Sawtimber volume on timberland by selected species, Minnesota 1977, 1990, 2003.

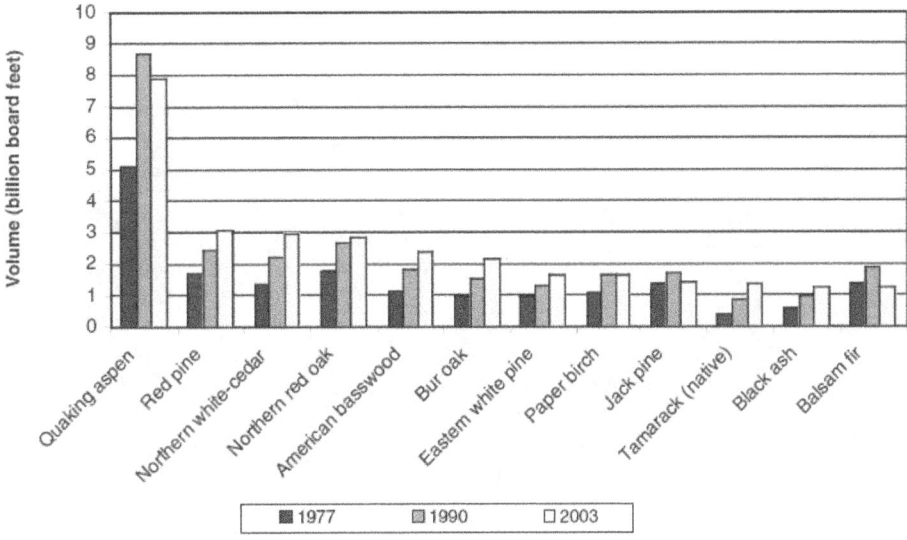

Figure 3.13. Sawtimber volume on timberland by major species group and tree grade, Minnesota, 2003.

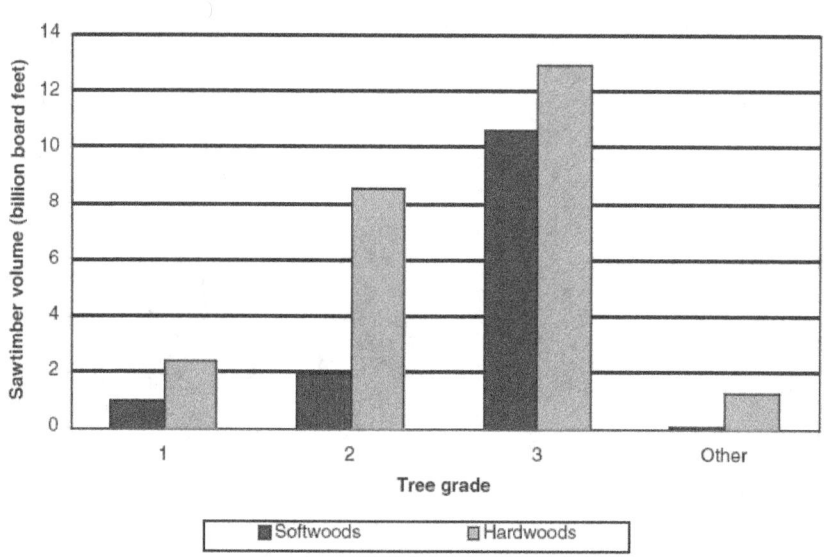

Stocking and Stand-Size Class

Background:

The density and size of stands across Minnesota provide information on the stages of stand development and forest stocking levels. Determining the stages of stand development helps us assess and predict the future growth and mortality of forest resources. Stocking is based on a combination of the number of trees, species, sizes, and spacing. A fully stocked stand indicates full use of the site. In stands of trees more than 5 inches in diameter, a fully stocked stand would typically have a basal area of more than 80 square feet per acre (where basal area is the cross-sectional area of tree stems measured at d.b.h.). In a seedling-sapling stand, a fully stocked stand would indicate the present number of trees is sufficient to attain a basal area of 80 square feet per acre when the trees are more than 5 inches in diameter.

What We Found:

Just over half (53 percent) of the forest land in Minnesota is fully stocked or overstocked, 33 percent is medium stocked, and 14 percent is poorly stocked or nonstocked. There is no discernible pattern to the spatial distribution of stocking within the State. The proportion of seedling-sapling stands that are overstocked or fully stocked is 69 percent, followed by large diameter stands (52 percent) and medium diameter stands (42 percent).

Stocking levels vary by forest type (fig. 3.14). Aspen forest land is nearly 66 percent fully or overstocked; tamarack is only 33 percent fully or overstocked. Stocking is generally lower on low-lying forest types.

The forests of Minnesota are fairly evenly split between the three main stand-size classes. Large-diameter stands (where most of the stocking is in hardwoods 11 inches d.b.h. and larger and softwoods 9 inches d.b.h. and larger) are found on 27 percent of Minnesota's forests. Seedling-sapling stands, where most of the stocking is in trees less than 5 inches d.b.h., occupy 33 percent of the forest land. Medium-diameter stands, where most of the stocking is in softwood trees from 5 inches to 9 inches and hardwood trees from 5 to 11 inches, occupy 38 percent of the forest land in Minnesota. The proportion of land area in each of the stand-size classes varies considerably by forest type (fig. 3.15). Almost 68 percent of the oak forest type is in the large-diameter stand-size class. At the other end of the spectrum are tamarack and black spruce with less than 10 percent stocking in the large-diameter class.

What This Means:

The low proportion of small-diameter oak stands points to the difficulties in regenerating oak. Poor oak regeneration is generally tied to the cumulative impact of human actions and interventions. For instance, recurrent fire is important for oak regeneration because it eliminates many of the oak's competitors. However, because of fire suppression, non-oaks are taking over oak stands. For oaks to remain a viable component of Minnesota's forests, more active management of woodlots to promote oak regeneration will be necessary.

Low stocking-levels and a high proportion of small-diameter stands for tamarack and black spruce are to be expected given the generally low site productivity of areas occupied by these lowland types. Of more concern is the small proportion of the northern white-cedar type in small-diameter stands, which also points to regeneration problems. Regeneration in northern white-cedar is often hindered by animal browsing.

All-live basal area per acre of timberland has been remarkably constant over the last quarter century. In 1977 the weighted average basal area was 78 square feet per acre; in 2003 the weighted average was 79 square feet per acre.

35

Figure 3.14. Percentage of forest land area by stocking class for each forest type, Minnesota, 2003.

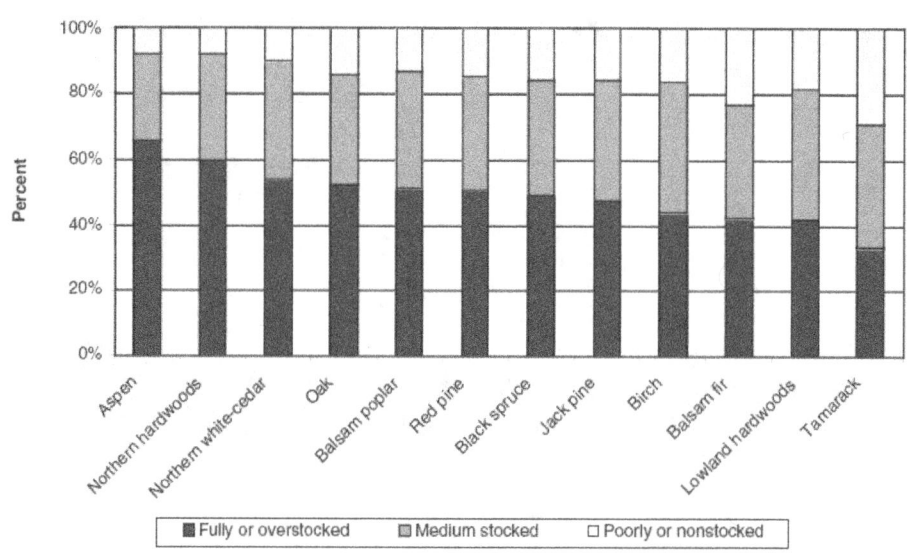

Figure 3.15. Percentage of forest land area by stand-size class for each forest type, Minnesota, 2003.

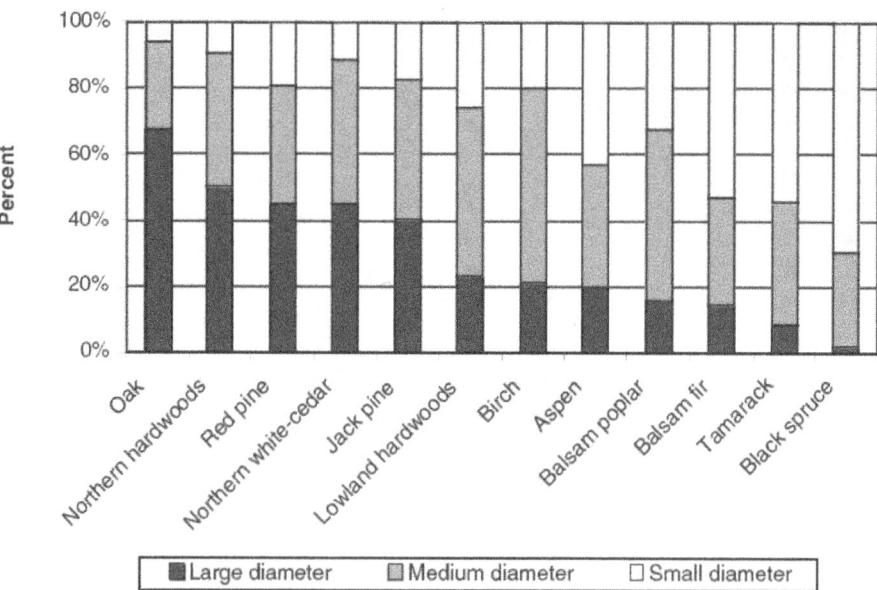

Average Annual Net Growth

Background:

Growth is computed by measuring trees at two points in time and determining the average annual change in volume over the period. If the volume on a plot increased from 1990 to 2003, then a net increase in growth would be reported. If the volume declined due to mortality, then there would be a net decrease in growth. The total volume change divided by the number of years between measurements would yield the net average annual growth on the plot.

What We Found:

The average annual net growth for Minnesota in 1990-2002 was 404 million cubic feet or roughly 2.6 percent of the total growing-stock volume in 2003. Growth expressed as a percent of volume is presented for the 12 most abundant (by cubic foot volume) species in Minnesota in 2003 (fig. 3.16). The growth rate for bur oak was the greatest at 4.7 percent; the growth rate for paper birch was negative due to excessive mortality rates.

The growth rate as a percent of volume varies by landowner class. The rate is highest for private landowners (3.3 percent) followed by State and local governments (2.2 percent) and national forests (1.5 percent). The distribution of growth is shown in figure 3.17, where 160,000-acre hexagons were used to plot the rate of growth. The hexagon coverage originally created by the Environmental Protection Agency's EMAP project, is often used to display coarse data that cannot be displayed at finer scales. Hexagons with negative net growth rates, where mortality actually exceeded gross growth, are shaded light yellow. Hexagons with low growth rates (from 0 to 1 percent of growing-stock volume) are shaded dark yellow. Hexagons with moderate growth rates (from 1 to 3 percent of current growing-stock volume) are shaded light green, and hexagons where average annual net growth exceeded 3 percent of current growing-stock volume are shaded dark green. A nonforest mask was placed over the hexagons to more fairly represent the area from which growth could have been obtained.

What This Means:

Growth rates are useful indicators of sustainability, disturbance trends, species vitality, and direction of succession. But growth provides only one piece of the sustainability puzzle. Information on mortality and removals is also needed to identify the changing composition of the forest. The three change components (growth, mortality, and removals) provide information only on trees greater than 5 inches in diameter. As a result, information on the understory component is not reflected in any of these measures.

Still, the growth rates in Minnesota are promising. The average annual net growth rate from 1977 to 1989 was 370 million cubic feet. By 1990 to 2002, this had increased to 404 million cubic feet.

Figure 3.16. Average annual net growth of growing stock on timberland as a percent of volume for the 12 most abundant species in Minnesota, 1990-2002.

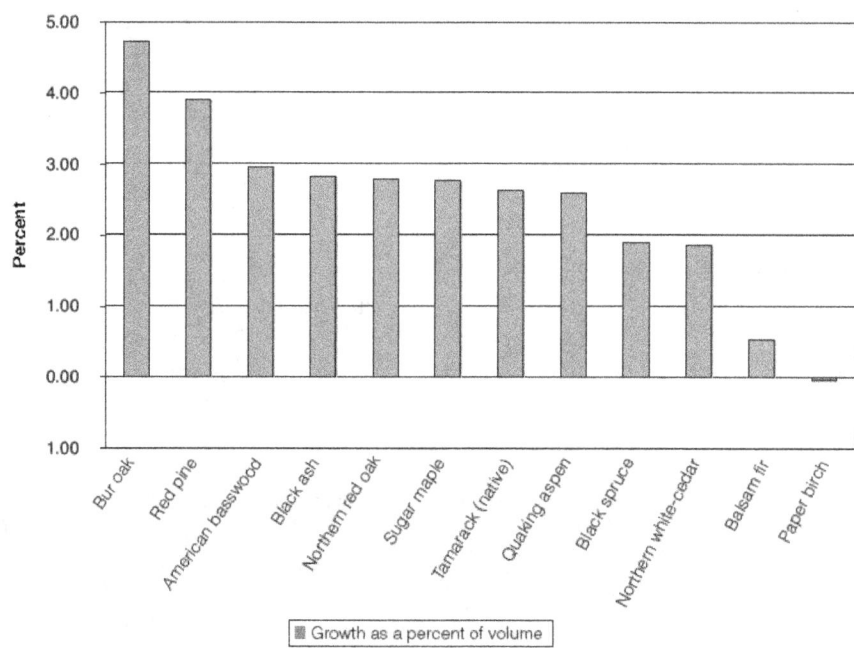

Figure 3.17. Average annual growing-stock growth rates, Minnesota, 1990-2002.

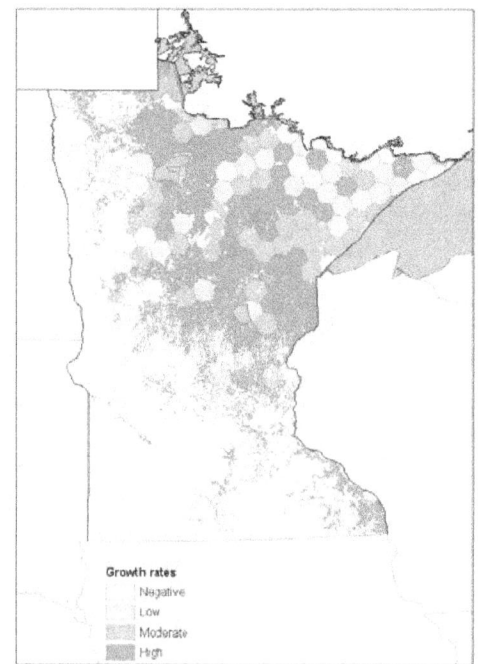

Average Annual Mortality

Background:

Mortality occurs as a result of adverse weather, disease, insects (native and exotic), senescence, competition, succession, fire, and human and animal activity. Trees killed as a result of harvesting or land clearing are considered removals and are not included in mortality.

What We Found:

The average annual growing-stock mortality for Minnesota in 1990-2002 was 272 million cubic feet or roughly 1.8 percent of the 2003 volume. Mortality expressed as a percent of volume is presented for the 12 most abundant (by cubic foot volume) species in Minnesota in 2003 (fig. 3.18). The mortality rate for balsam fir was the greatest at 5.6 percent; the mortality rate for bur oak was the lowest at 0.2 percent.

The primary cause of mortality could not be determined in more than two-thirds of the cases, which is not surprising considering that some of the trees had died more than 13 years ago soon after the completion of the previous inventory.

Among the various identifiable primary causes of tree mortality were weather, disease, and animal and insect damage. While insects were responsible for only a small percentage of the primary cause of mortality, they contributed to a much greater share of it by weakening trees and making them vulnerable to disease and other forms of attack.

Mortality rates increased from 208 million cubic feet per year in 1990 to 272 million cubic feet per year in 2003. The average annual mortality reported in 2003 expressed as a percentage of the 2003 volume is 1.8 percent, which is significantly higher than the rate reported for the 1977 inventory (1.2 percent) or for the 1990 inventory (1.3 percent). The rate of 1.8 percent is also significantly higher than the mortality rates for two neighboring States, Iowa (0.8 percent) and Wisconsin (0.9 percent).

The mortality rate as a percent of volume varies by landowner class. The rate is highest for national forests (2.1 percent) followed by State and local governments (1.9 percent) and private landowners (1.5 percent). The spatial distribution of mortality is presented in figure 3.19 where 160,000-acre hexagons were used to plot the rate of mortality. Hexagons with low mortality rates, where average annual growing-stock mortality is less than 1 percent of current growing stock, are shaded yellow. Hexagons with moderate mortality rates (from 1 to 3 percent of current growing-stock volume) are shaded light green, and hexagons where average annual mortality exceeded 3 percent of current growing-stock volume are shaded dark green. A nonforest mask (based on NLCD coverage) was placed over the hexagons to more fairly represent the area from which mortality could have been obtained, i.e., those areas classified as nonforest in the NLCD are colored white in the figure.

What This Means:

Some of the increase in mortality may be due to the increasing age of Minnesota's forests and natural mortality patterns during stand development/succession. Single large weather events also contributed to the increase in mortality. The July 4, 1999, blowdown caused serious damage to thousands of acres of forests in northeastern Minnesota. Even events going all the way back to the drought of 1988 may have weakened trees enough to make them susceptible to insects and diseases during 1990 to 2002.

Figure 3.18. Average annual mortality of growing stock on timberland as a percent of volume for the 12 most abundant species in Minnesota, 1990-2002.

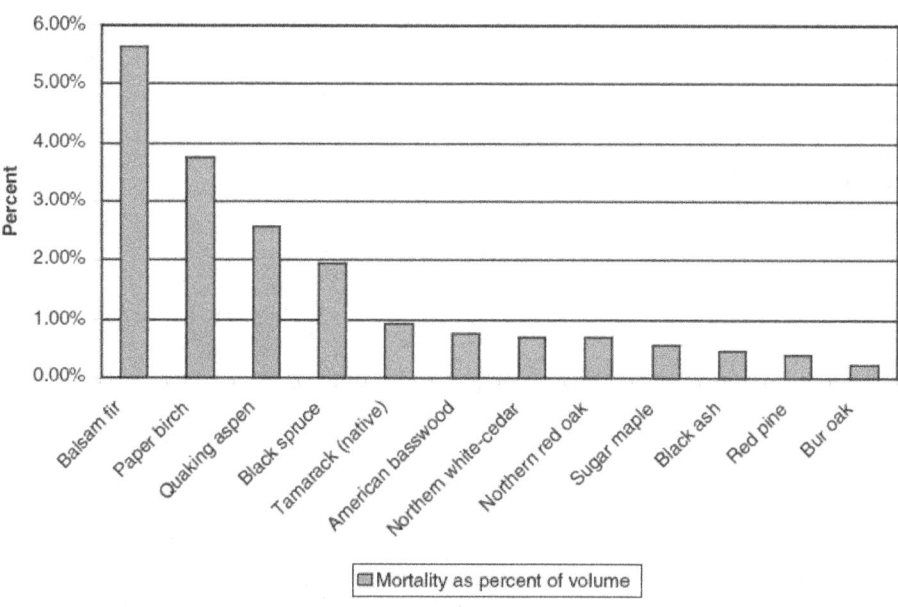

Figure 3.19. Average annual growing-stock mortality rates, Minnesota, 1990-2002.

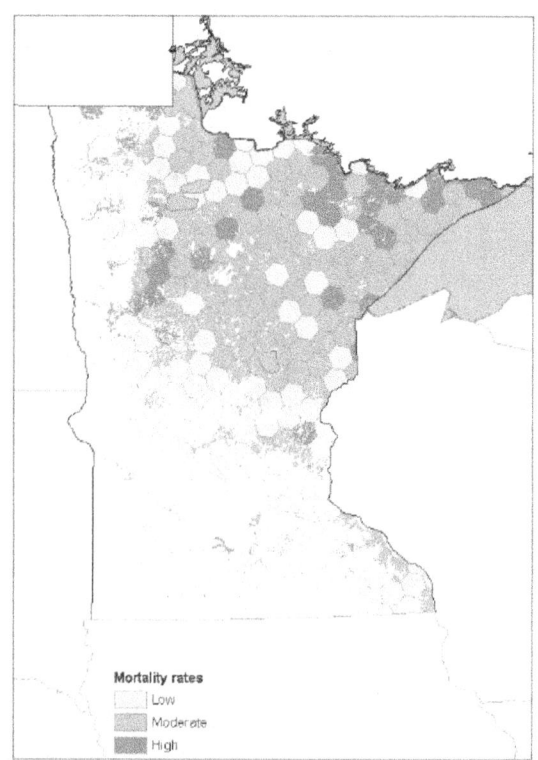

Average Annual Removals

Background: There are three types of removals: (1) harvest removals, (2) mortality removals (trees killed during the harvesting process and left on the land), and (3) diversion removals (living trees previously on land classified as timberland now on land classified as nontimberland—removed from the timberland base due to land use change).

What We Found: The average annual growing-stock removals for Minnesota from 1990 to 2002 was 249 million cubic feet or roughly 1.6 percent of the total growing-stock volume in 2003. Removals expressed as a percent of volume is presented for the 12 most abundant (by volume) species in Minnesota in 2003 (fig. 3.20). The removals rate for quaking aspen was the greatest at 3.3 percent; the removals rate for sugar maple was the lowest at 0.3 percent.

Other significant species (at least 100 million cubic feet growing-stock volume) with high removals rates include jack pine (3.9 percent), eastern cottonwood (2.9 percent), and balsam poplar (2.5 percent). Significant species with low removals rates include green ash (0.6 percent), silver maple (0.6 percent), and American elm (0.7 percent).

The removals rate as a percent of volume varies by landowner class. The rate is highest for State and local governments (1.8 percent) followed by private landowners (1.6 percent) and the national forests (1.2 percent). The spatial distribution of removals is presented in figure 3.21 where 160,000-acre hexagons were used to plot the rate of removals. Hexagons with low removals rates, where average annual growing-stock removals is less than 1 percent of current growing stock, are shaded yellow. Hexagons with moderate removals rates (from 1 to 3 percent of current growing-stock volume) are shaded light green, and hexagons where average annual removals exceeded 3 percent of current growing-stock volume are shaded dark green. A nonforest mask was placed over the hexagons to more fairly represent the area from which removals could have been obtained.

Most (92 percent) of the removals in Minnesota over 1990-2002, as measured from FIA field plots, was due to harvesting. Eighty-eight percent of the removals was cut and used while 4 percent was killed as a result of harvesting and left in the forest (fig. 3.22). The remaining 8 percent was diversion removals due to land use change where trees were left standing but the land they were on was reclassified from timberland to nontimberland.

Figure 3.20. Average annual removals of growing stock on timberland as a percent of volume for the 12 most abundant species in Minnesota, 1990-2002.

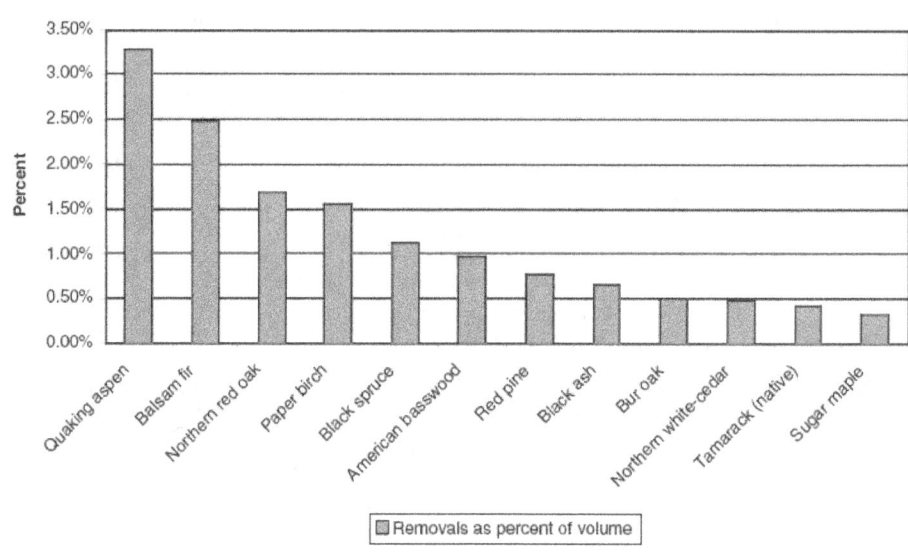

Figure 3.21. Average annual growing-stock removals rates, Minnesota, 1990-2002.

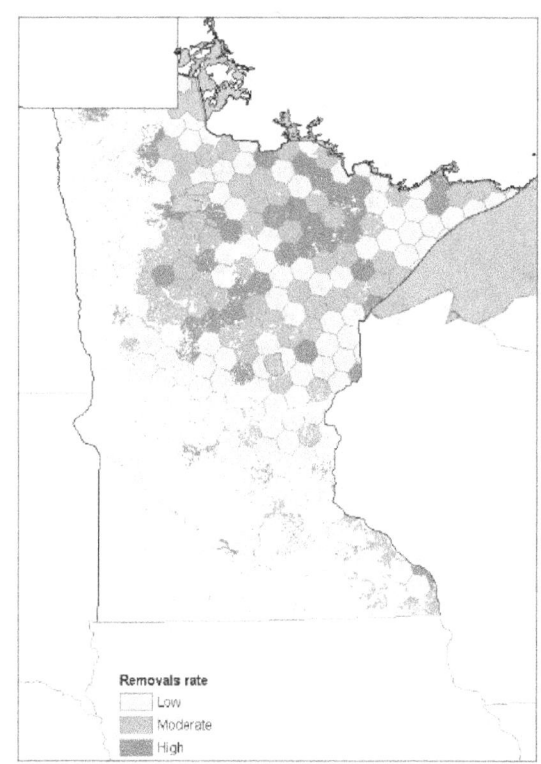

Figure 3.22. Average annual growing-stock removals from timberland by disposition of timber, Minnesota, 1990-2002.

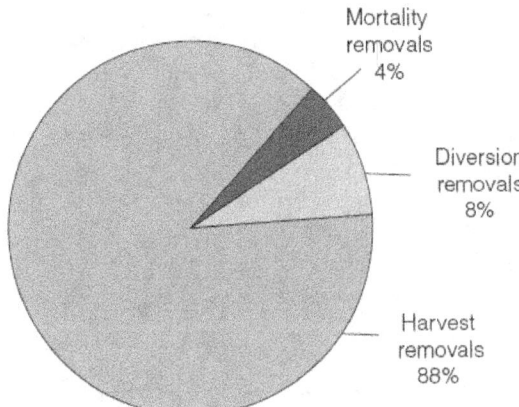

Mortality removals 4%

Diversion removals 8%

Harvest removals 88%

Growth to Removals Ratio

One measure of sustainability is the growth to removals ratio (G/R). A number greater than 1.0 indicates the volume of the species is increasing. A number less than 1 indicates the volume is decreasing. Overall, the G/R for 1990 to 2003 was 1.6 indicating that overall volume was indeed increasing. On a species by species basis, the picture is less clear (fig. 3.23). Bur oak has a G/R of more than 9; paper birch has a negative G/R because its mortality exceeds its gross growth, resulting in a negative net growth.

To achieve management goals, it makes sense at times to manage the forest so that a species will temporarily have a G/R ratio of less than 1.0. When short-lived species such as quaking aspen are nearing senescence, it may make sense to try to "capture mortality" (harvest a tree before it dies of old age).

The average annual removals of growing stock reported for 1990 to 2002 (249 million cubic feet) was slightly lower than the 261 million cubic feet reported for the previous period (1977 to 1989). Of the three components of change (growth, removals, and mortality), removals is the most directly tied to human activity and is thus the most responsive to changing economic conditions.

What This Means:

Bug infestations, disease, and succession can result in low G/R ratios. Paper birch had a negative G/R due to mortality actually exceeding gross growth over the period. High mortality rates for balsam fir due to spruce budworm infestations were partially responsible for a low G/R ratio.

The G/R for all species is a healthy 1.6 statewide. Some of the decrease in removals may be due to increasing imports from Wisconsin and Canada (Jacobson 2004).

Figure 3.23. Ratio of average annual net growth to average annual removals for the 12 most abundant species in Minnesota, 1990-2002.

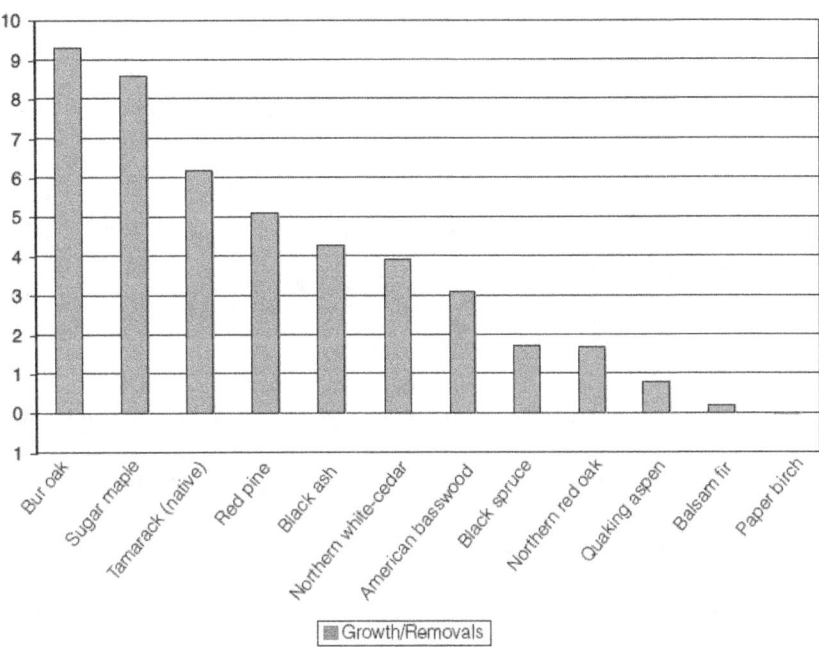

Growth/Removals

Forest Health

Forest Health Indicators

Tree Crowns

Background:

The overall condition of tree crowns within a forest stand may indicate the health status of forests. For example, a forest suffering from a disease epidemic will have obvious dieback, low crown ratios, and high transparency.

What We Found:

Dieback is measured as the percent of branch tips in the crown that are dead. The categories for the dieback indicator are none (0-5 percent), light (6-20 percent), moderate (21-50 percent), and severe (51-100 percent). Overall, 92 percent of the trees had no dieback, 7 percent had light dieback, and only 1 percent had moderate or severe dieback. The ash species group is the most susceptible to dieback: 15 percent of the trees had light dieback and 3 percent had moderate to severe dieback (fig. 4.1).

The crown ratio of a tree is defined as the portion of the tree height supporting live foliage. The spruce and balsam fir species group has the highest mean crown ratio at just over 70 percent. The black walnut and cottonwood and aspen species groups have the lowest mean crown ratios at something less than 40 percent. Crown transparency is a measure of the proportion of the crown through which the sky is visible. The cottonwood and aspen species group has the highest average crown transparency, approaching 30 percent; the hickory species group has an average crown transparency of only 15 percent.

What This Means:

Means of the crown indicators by species group appear to indicate there are no major health problems with crown conditions in Minnesota. Trend data are needed to develop a baseline for crown health. Crown ratio and crown transparency appear to be inversely related: the higher the crown ratio the lower the transparency. Crown ratios are generally higher for trees on the edge of the forest. Increased forest fragmentation may therefore result in higher average crown ratios.

Figure 4.1. Percentages of dieback (moderate to severe), mean crown transparency, and mean uncompacted crown ratio for selected species groups, Minnesota, 2003.

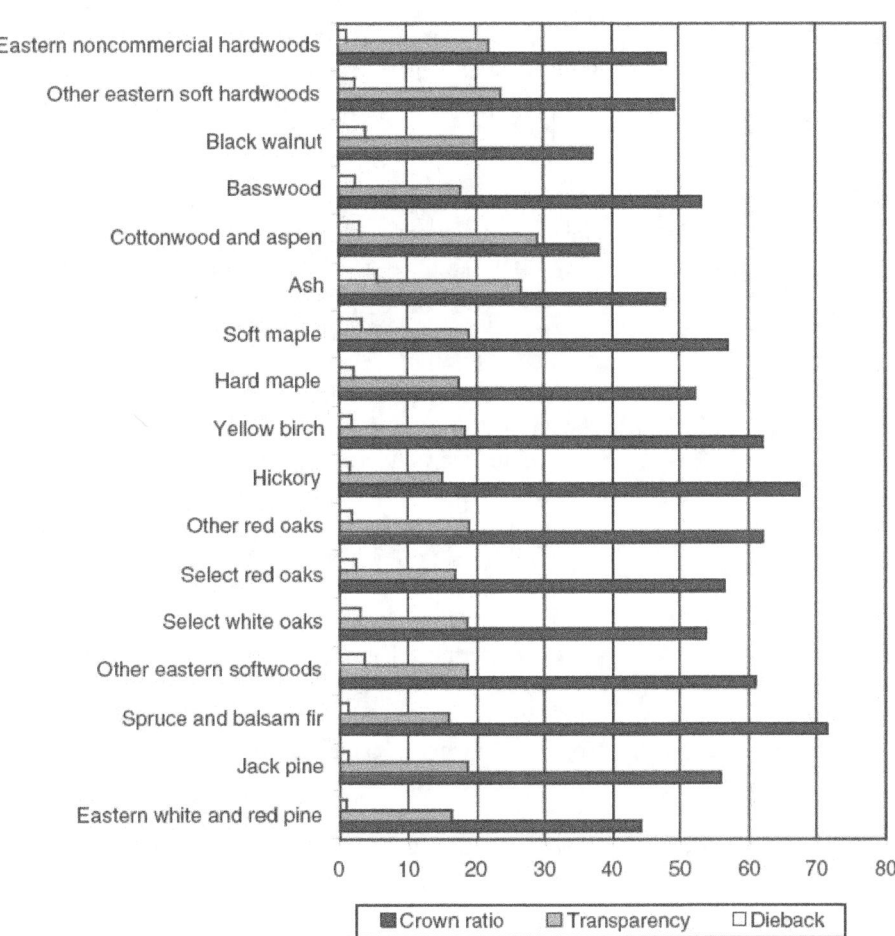

Down Woody Debris

Background:

Down woody debris, in the form of fallen trees, branches, litter fall, and duff, fulfills a critical ecological niche in Minnesota's forests. Down woody debris provides valuable wildlife habitat, largely determines forest fire behavior, and is an important carbon sink.

What We Found:

The fuel loadings of down woody materials (a component of fire hazard) are not exceedingly high in Minnesota (fig. 4.2). When compared to neighboring Wisconsin and Michigan, Minnesota's loadings of the smaller-sized fuels (1-hr and 10-hr) are not significantly different. However, the loadings of the largest fuels (100- and 1,000+-hr) are significantly greater for Minnesota than for Wisconsin and Michigan. There is no apparent trend in total down woody fuel loadings (fine and coarse woody debris) among classes of live tree density, although the lowest fuel loadings are associated with the highest levels of standing tree density (fig. 4.3). The size-class distribution of coarse woody debris appears to be heavily skewed (84 percent) toward pieces less than 8 inches in diameter at point of intersection with plot sampling planes (fig. 4.4). The stages of coarse woody decay (fig. 4.5) appear to be fairly uniformly distributed. The highest coarse woody debris volumes can be found in the BWCAW, Duluth areas, and along prairie/forest intermixes (fig. 4.6).

What This Means:

During the sampling timeframe of 2001-2003, the effects of the BWCAW blowdown were still being seen in the higher amounts of larger down woody fuels in Minnesota compared to neighboring States. Additionally, a higher proportion of freshly fallen (decay classes 1 and 2) coarse woody pieces can be found in Minnesota, as compared to most other regions of the U.S. The BWCAW blowdown has also obscured relationships between down dead materials and standing tree density. Areas unaffected by blowdowns may often have higher fuel loadings in mature stands (high density). In contrast, areas in recently wind-damaged stands may have very little standing tree density because most of the recently living trees are now down woody material. High coarse woody tree volumes can arise only through tree mortality, whether through stand development or disturbances. From the spatial distribution of coarse woody volumes across Minnesota, it appears as though areas affected by wind disturbances typically have higher coarse woody volumes (i.e., BWCAW and prairie border forests). Overall, because fuel loadings are not exceedingly high across Minnesota, possible fire dangers are outweighed by the wildlife habitat benefit provided by Minnesota's diverse down woody habitats.

Figure 4.2. Estimates of mean fuel loadings (tons/acre) by fuel-hour class for Minnesota, Michigan, and Wisconsin (error bars represent one standard error).

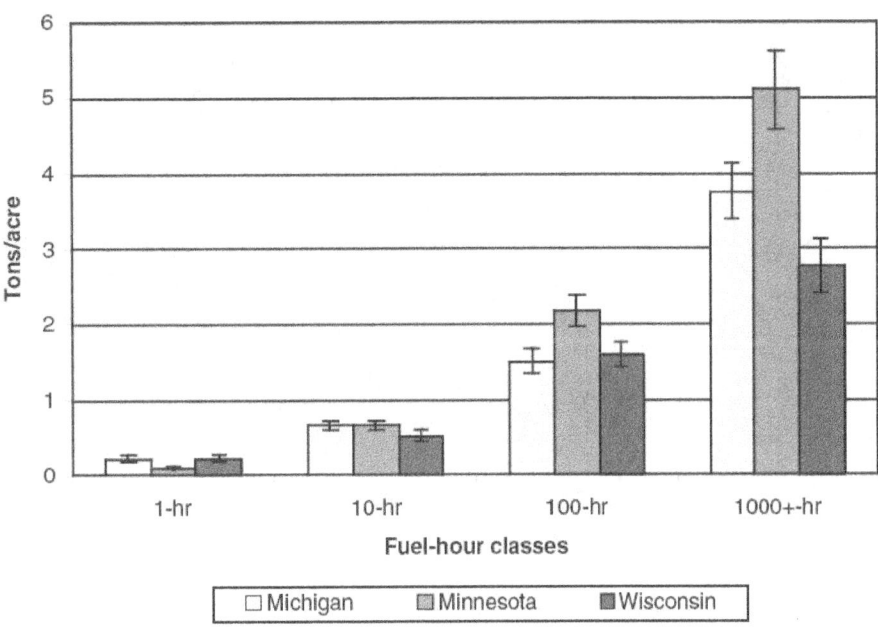

Figure 4.3. Estimates of mean down woody fuels (tons/acre, fine and coarse woody debris) by stand density (basal area/acre), Minnesota, 2001-2003 (error bars represent one standard error).

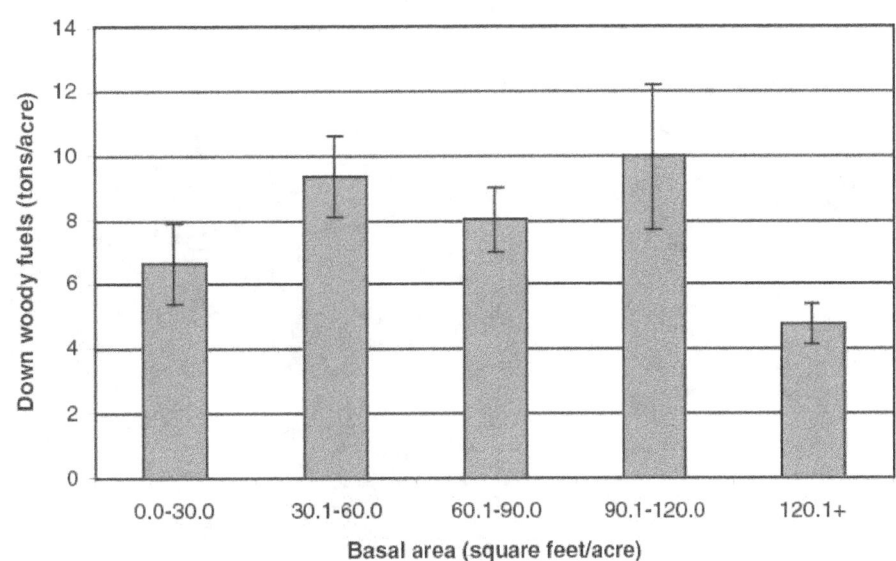

Figure 4.4. Mean distribution of coarse woody debris (pieces per acre) by size class, Minnesota, 2001-2003.

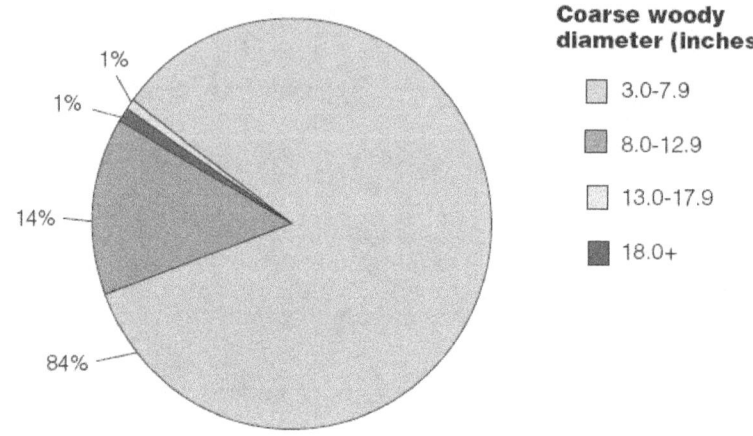

Coarse woody diameter (inches)

- ☐ 3.0-7.9
- ☐ 8.0-12.9
- ☐ 13.0-17.9
- ■ 18.0+

Figure 4.5. Mean distribution of coarse woody debris (pieces per acre) by decay class (1=least decayed...5=most decayed), Minnesota, 2001-2003.

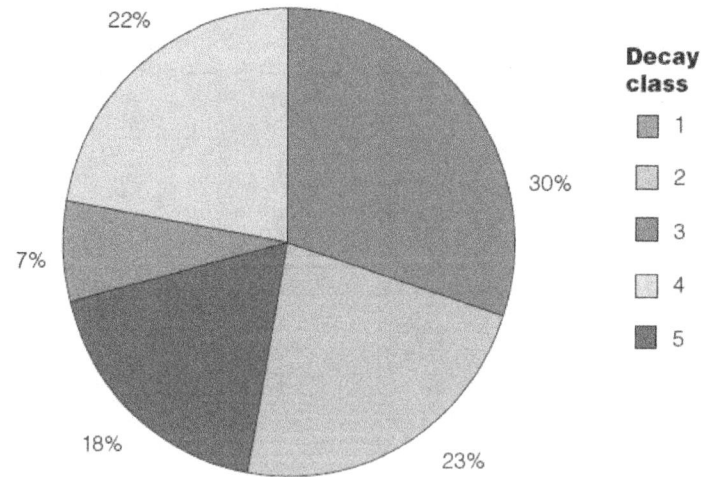

Decay class

- 1
- 2
- 3
- 4
- 5

Figure 4.6. Volumes (interpolated) of coarse woody debris (cubic feet/acre), Minnesota, 2001-2003.

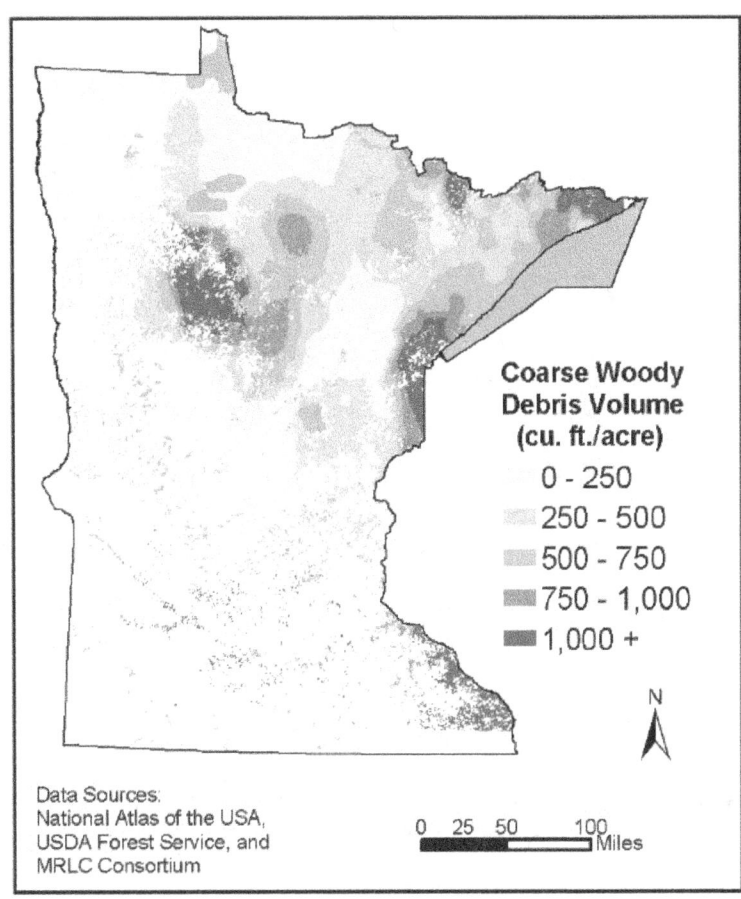

Ozone Damage

Background:

Bioindicator leaf injury surveys were initiated in Minnesota in 1994. Minnesota has 27 permanent biosites scattered across the State, and foliar injury symptoms have been observed on only a few of these sites.

What We Found:

Ground level ozone exposures in Minnesota are among the lowest of the North Central States. They typically fall below thresholds that would result in significant foliar injury, growth loss, or adverse long-term consequences on the majority of forest species (fig. 4.7). However, ozone occasionally reaches hourly concentrations and seasonal cumulative values high enough to cause foliar injury on the more sensitive bioindicator species (fig. 4.8).

The forest areas in northern Minnesota are at lowest risk of ozone injury. Ozone-sensitive species in southeastern and south-central Minnesota, particularly downwind of the Twin Cities, are at modest risk of ozone impacts. However, quantifying the effects is difficult because of other critical growth and health variables such as drought, insects, diseases, competition, and invasive species.

Minnesota ozone exposures are modest compared to the serious ozone pollution generated in the Chicago and St. Louis metropolitan areas. But peak hourly ozone values in the Twin Cities area exceeded 100 parts per billion during the 1998-2002 period. Peak hourly ozone values over 100 parts per billion and some seasonal exposure exceeded thresholds suggested by the interagency Federal Land Managers Air Quality Group.

What This Means:

Minnesota's forests, particularly in the south, are exposed to peak and seasonal cumulative ozone concentrations considered above background levels. These exposures, however, are not sufficient to generally result in substantial impacts that can be either seen or measured. Consequently, ozone impacts are considered a low risk over the vast majority of the State. Ozone-sensitive species in the eastern part of Minnesota near the Twin Cities are at the most risk of injury during the occasional summer with above average ozone concentrations.

Figure 4.7. Ozone exposure levels, United States, 1999-2003.

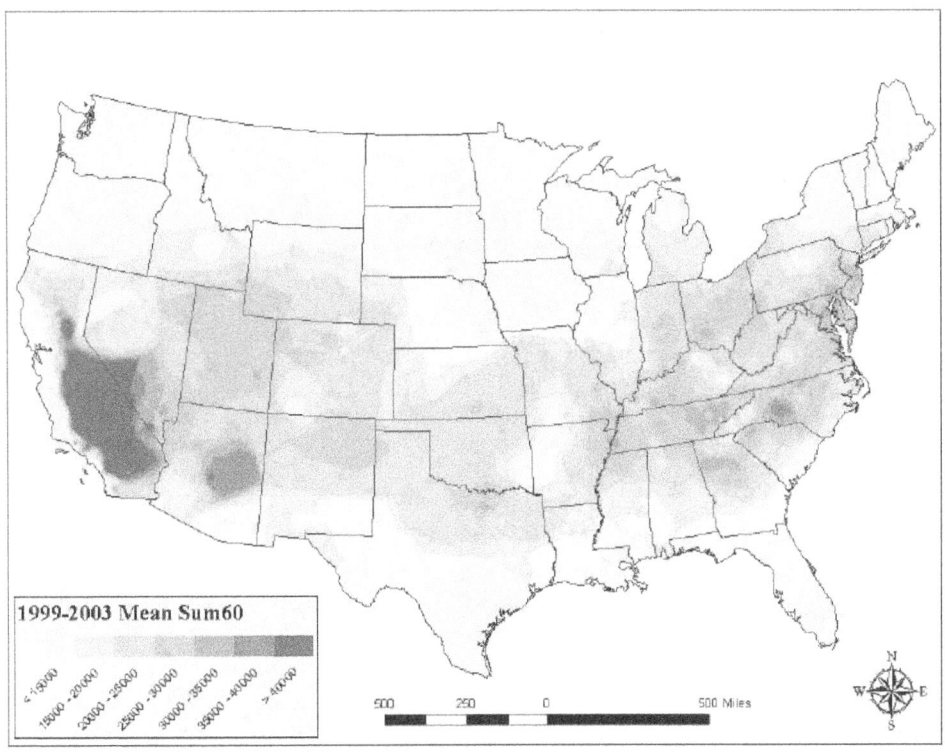

Figure 4.8. Ozone injury.

Forest Soils

Background:

Rich soils are the foundation of productive forest land. Inventory and assessment of the forest soil resource provides critical baseline information on forest health and productivity, especially in light of continued natural and human disturbance.

What We Found:

The forests of Minnesota are largely underlain by alfisols, inceptisols, entisols, and histosols (fig. 4.9). Alfisols are fertile soils generally developed under deciduous forest (Brady 1990). Inceptisols are a very diverse soil occurring across a range of climates and vegetative communities. Inceptisols are weakly developed soils. Entisols are young soils, common in river bottoms and outwash sands (Anderson et al. 2001). Histosols are the marsh and bog soils found in ancient glacial lakebeds across northern Minnesota (Anderson et al. 2001).

Field data were collected from 2001 to 2003. The paucity of data makes it difficult to compare soils under different forest type groups. Here, only forest type groups with more than five samples are considered.

The forest floors under coniferous forest-type groups are thicker than those under deciduous ones (fig. 4.10). The spruce/fir forest-type group also has a higher relative carbon content (fig. 4.11). Conversely, the coniferous forest-type groups have lower soil pH (0-10 cm) than the deciduous forest-type groups (fig. 4.12). The white/red/jack pine forest-type group appears to occur on the poorest quality sites. Effective cation exchange capacity (ECEC) is a measure of the soil's fertility related to its ability to hold onto nutrients and prevent them from leaching as water leaches through the soil profile. Calcium and the other nutrients summarized by ECEC are lowest in the white/red/jack pine forest-type group, and aluminum levels are the highest in this forest-type group (table 4.1). Aluminum can be toxic under certain conditions.

Soil quality index (SQI) is a new index designed to integrate the distinct physical and chemical properties of the soil into a single assessment (Amacher and O'Neill, in prep). The lowest SQI values in the State occur in the arrowhead region, but the overall average is moderated by adjacent soils of higher quality (fig. 4.13). Higher quality soils are found in the forest/prairie transition zone. Higher amounts of soil carbon are observed in the ancient glacial lakebeds of northwestern Minnesota (fig. 4.14).

What This Means:

Conifer forests tend to accumulate greater amounts of forest floor than deciduous stands. This results from the chemical properties of the litter itself; conifer needles tend to have lower nutrient content and thus break down more slowly than deciduous leaves (Pritchett and Fisher 1987). The lesser accumulations of forest floor under deciduous stands may also be related to worm outbreaks that consume deciduous litter (Hale et al. 2005). This is known to adversely affect rare plants (Gundale 2002), nutrient cycling (Bohlen et al. 2004a), and the broader plant community (Bohlen et al. 2004b).

The low soil pH, high aluminum, and low ECEC are all related to the chemistry of the coniferous litter. Coniferous litter is more acidic than deciduous litter (Pritchett and Fisher 1987), so low pH leachate percolates through the soil profile. The hydrogen ions tend to displace the native minerals useful for plant growth and lower the pH of the mineral soil (Brady 1990). Aluminum is increasingly mobilized as soil pH decreases (McBride 1994).

Figure 4.9. The forests of Minnesota are concentrated on alfisols and inceptisols in the northeastern corner of the State. Entisols and histosols are also prominent forest soils.

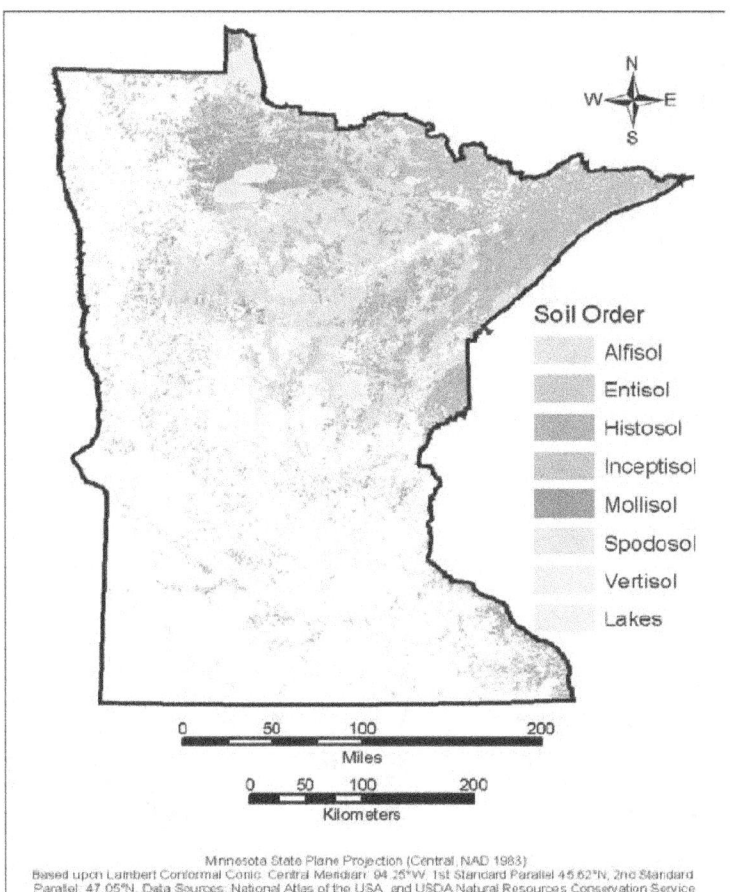

Figure 4.10. Thickness of forest floor under various forest type groups. (Data are from 2001 to 2003. Error bars represent one standard error.)

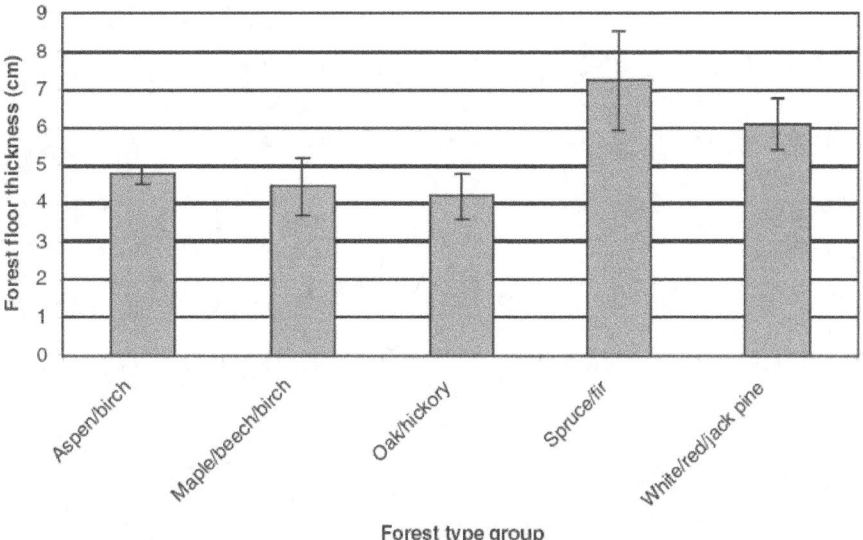

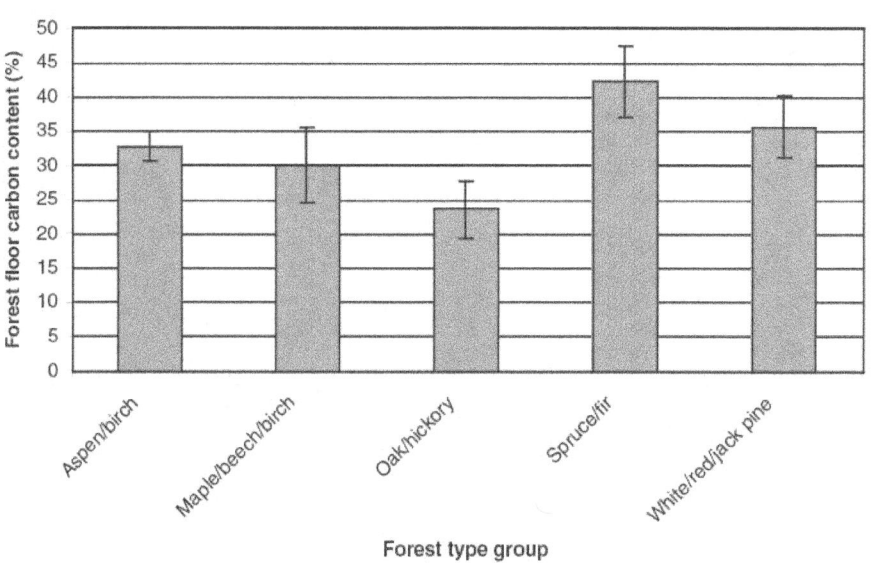

Figure 4.11. Relative carbon content of the forest floor under various forest type groups. (Data are from 2001 to 2003. Error bars represent one standard error.)

Table 4.1. Selected chemical properties of the mineral soil, Minnesota, 2001-2003

Soil Layer and forest type group	No. of samples	Sodium	Potassium	Calcium	Magnesium	Aluminum	ECEC
		- (mg/ha) -					
Mineral (0-10 cm)							
Aspen/birch	43	16.88	146.53	1,519.01	256.50	77.09	10.99
Maple/beech/birch	6	22.78	188.43	2,247.65	348.17	175.83	16.61
Oak/hickory	8	12.35	109.06	1,817.55	258.74	4.48	11.58
Spruce/fir	9	15.52	83.03	1,202.17	157.21	213.53	9.95
White/red/jack pine	9	16.58	93.50	655.85	100.83	271.24	7.43
Mineral (10-20 cm)							
Aspen/birch	39	13.50	62.66	807.27	143.84	96.15	6.50
Maple/beech/birch	4	17.47	132.93	2,741.40	458.00	83.47	18.79
Oak/hickory	8	11.90	43.58	787.16	121.03	25.00	5.36
Spruce/fir	7	17.00	62.18	1,302.97	181.59	126.84	9.63
White/red/jack pine	7	14.06	39.32	454.47	76.99	55.33	3.68

Figure 4.12. Soil pH in the surface soil (0-10 cm). (Data are from 2001 to 2003. Error bars represent one standard error.)

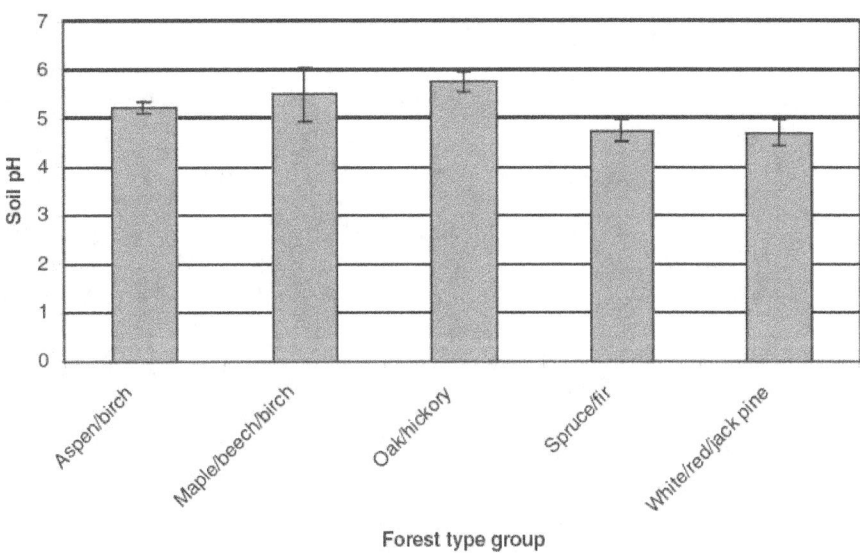

Figure 4.13. Soil quality index values for plots and averaged across Major Land Resource Areas (MLRAs), Minnesota, 2001-2003.

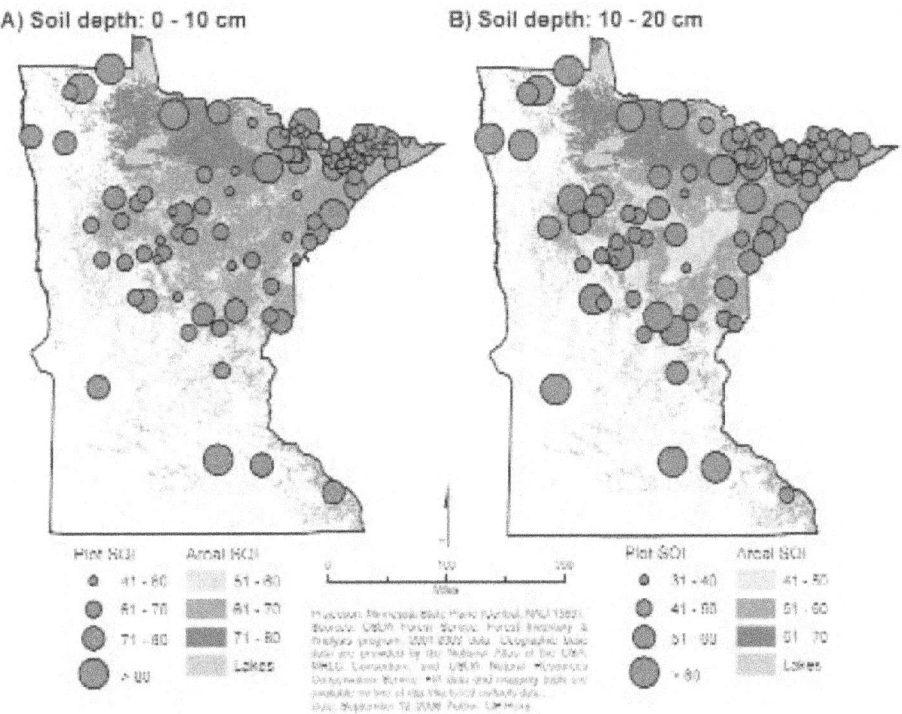

Figure 4.14. Soil carbon sequestration observed on plots and averaged across Major Land Resource Areas (MLRAs), Minnesota, 2001-2003.

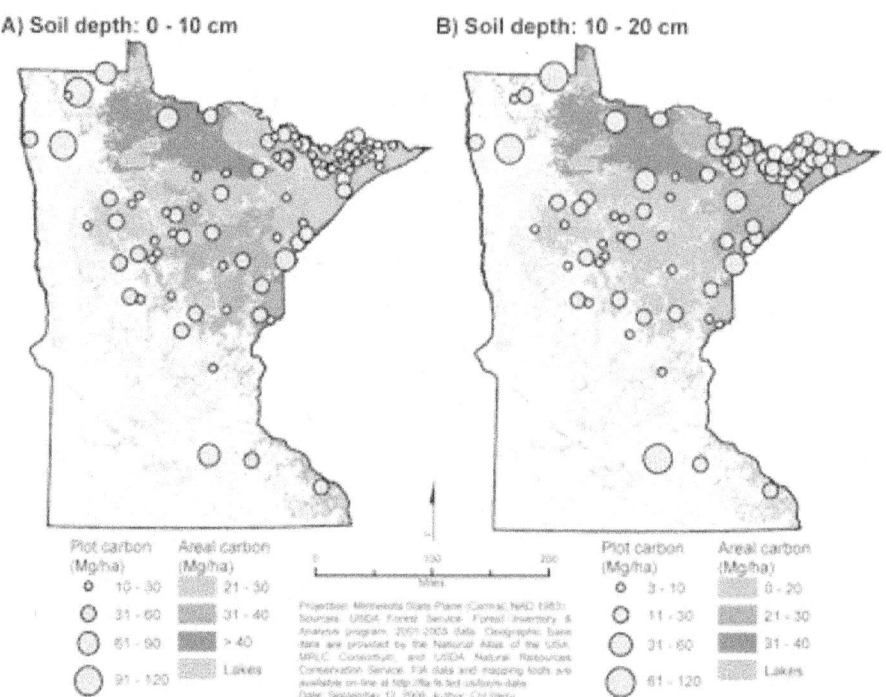

Forest Insects and Disease

Background:

During the past decades, exotic/invasive insects and diseases have had a large impact on Minnesota's forest health. Diseases such as white pine blister rust and Dutch elm disease greatly altered the health and makeup of Minnesota's forests over the last century. Monitoring insects and diseases in the context of abiotic agents (e.g., drought) is crucial to predicting and managing Minnesota's future forest resources.

What We Found:

Insects, pathogens, weather, fire, and other factors cause damage and losses in forests throughout Minnesota every year. Since 1954 the eastern spruce budworm has defoliated spruce/fir forests annually, establishing itself as the most consistent damaging agent in the State. The prevalence of spruce budworm had been declining over most of the past decade, but it increased significantly in 2002 and then declined again in 2003 by 60 percent to 35 thousand acres. Another defoliator, the forest tent caterpillar, was active on a large scale throughout aspen and birch forests for the fifth consecutive year, although declining to 2.25 million acres, down from 7.4 million acres in 2002. Populations were expected to be much smaller in 2004 with only localized spots defoliated. Other significant damage agents active during 2003 were jack pine budworm defoliating 18,546 acres and killing older, open-growing jack pine; and the introduced larch casebearer defoliating larch on more than 1,660 acres, down by 40 percent from 2002.

Since 1997, all of these and other defoliating agents have been active, sometimes on some of the same land at the same time. Many trees that are repeatedly defoliated sustain measurable growth loss, which in turn, sometimes results in mortality. Figure 4.15 shows areas of the State where, since 1998, forested lands have been defoliated between one and four times.

Mortality from larch beetles declined by 50 percent in 2003 to just over 6,000 acres. Mortality is usually limited to individual trees or small pockets of trees. However, some stands of 30 acres and larger had more than 75 percent mortality.

In mid-August of 2002, two-lined chestnut borer damage began to show up in Itasca County. By late August, dieback, topkill, and whole tree mortality were widespread in northern and southern Minnesota. Stress from drought and 2 or more years of forest tent caterpillar defoliation likely contributed to the success of the borers. An aerial survey, flown in September 2003, detected mortality over an additional 12,557 acres in Cass, Itasca, northern Aitkin, northern Crow Wing, and southeastern Beltrami Counties.

Spruce beetle has been killing large-diameter white spruce along the Lake Superior shore over the past few years. The amount of mortality is increasing, and new infestations continue to be found. The damage is most obvious within a few miles of the lake, but has also been

found in Koochiching County as well as in a windbreak in Wadena County.

Oak wilt continues to be one of the greatest concerns in central Minnesota, especially in Sherburne and Anoka Counties. Following the storms of 1997 and 1998, the number of infection pockets dramatically increased in affected areas. As a result, the oak wilt

61

epicenter shifted northwestward into Sherburne County, where storm damage and increased development have put many oaks at risk. Some communities are making progress on reducing the number of centers, but overall, the incidence of oak wilt appears to be increasing.

What This Means:

Weather results in greater losses to the forests of Minnesota than insects and disease. But the combination of weather, insects, and disease is most lethal. Damage from high winds kills or wounds trees and provides habitat for beetles. Periods of drought and flood decrease the resistance of trees to insects and disease. But the combination of environmental stresses and endemic pathogens leads to periods of greater than average mortality. Future concerns, however, may lie not with sporadic outbreaks of mortality from resident pathogens but rather with new pests such as the European gypsy moth, emerald ash borer, and Sudden Oak Death.

Figure 4.15. Areas with high incidence of defoliation mapped by aerial survey, 1999-2003 (USDA Forest Service, Forest Health Protection, St. Paul Field Office).

# of years defoliated
0
1
2
3
4

Forest Change Issues

Land Use Change

Background:

Information on land use change is important for understanding the future direction of land use in Minnesota. The estimated area of forest land in presettlement times was 31.5 million acres (Marschner 1930). Most of the change in forest land area occurred before the first forest inventory in the 1930s. The focus here will be on the change in forest area between 1990 and 2003.

Minnesota Department of Natural Resources

What We Found:

Approximately 32 percent of Minnesota was forested in 2003. Thirty percent of the area of Minnesota remained forested over the entire period from 1990 to 2003 (fig 5.1). Two percent of Minnesota's area converted to forest land from nonforest land. Land that converts to forest land is typically referred to as reversions since it is assumed that at presettlement times the land had been forested and was now reverting back to its original land use. Sixty-eight percent of Minnesota was classified as nonforest in 2003. Sixty-five percent of Minnesota's area remained nonforest (land and water) over the entire period from 1990 to 2003. Three percent of the area of Minnesota converted from forest land to nonforest land. Land that converts from forest land to nonforest land is typically referred to as diversions.

Reversions—nonforest land that converted to forest land
Seventy percent of reversions come from two sources: marsh and water (39 percent) and farmland (31 percent) (fig. 5.2). The remaining 30 percent of reversions come from rights-of-way (11 percent), pasture and rangeland (9 percent), other lands with trees (8 percent), and urban forest land (2 percent).

Approximately 18 percent of the reversions from nonforest land to forest land were due to definitional changes introduced with the adoption of a national FIA field manual in 1999. The other land with trees (8 percent of reversions or 97 thousand acres) includes parks/golf courses/cemeteries/backyards. Most, if not all, of the land that had been classified as other land with trees in 1990 would have been classified as forest land using current definitions. In the 1990 inventory, wide windbreaks used to protect buildings (20 thousand acres) were called nonforest land even though they met all other requirements for forest. Most of the land classified as improved pasture and rangeland with trees in 1990 (111 thousand acres) would have been classified as forest land under current definitions.

Diversions—forest land that converted to nonforest land
Two-thirds of the losses to forest land were because of diversion to marsh and water (fig. 5.3). The other third of diversions were to urbanization (15 percent), pasture and rangeland (8 percent), farmland (5 percent), rights-of-way (3 percent), and urban forest land (2 percent).

What This Means:

The forest land area of Minnesota is, for the most part, fairly stable. Approximately 91 percent of the land forested in 1990 remained forested in 2003. About 9 percent of the area forested in 1990 diverted to nonforest land uses. But this was nearly offset by reversions to forest land equal to approximately 6 percent of the 1990 forest land area. The net effect was a 2.7-percent decrease in the area of forest land between 1990 and 2003. When the changes to the definition of forest land are considered, the estimate of the decrease in forest land is closer to 4 percent.

Low-lying areas appear to move between forest and nonforest classifications because of weather (drought/flooding) and other natural causes such as beaver dams. These conditions are often not permanent and therefore continued movement is likely. Other changes in land use are due primarily to socioeconomic factors.

Figure 5.1. Land use change, Minnesota, 1990-2003.

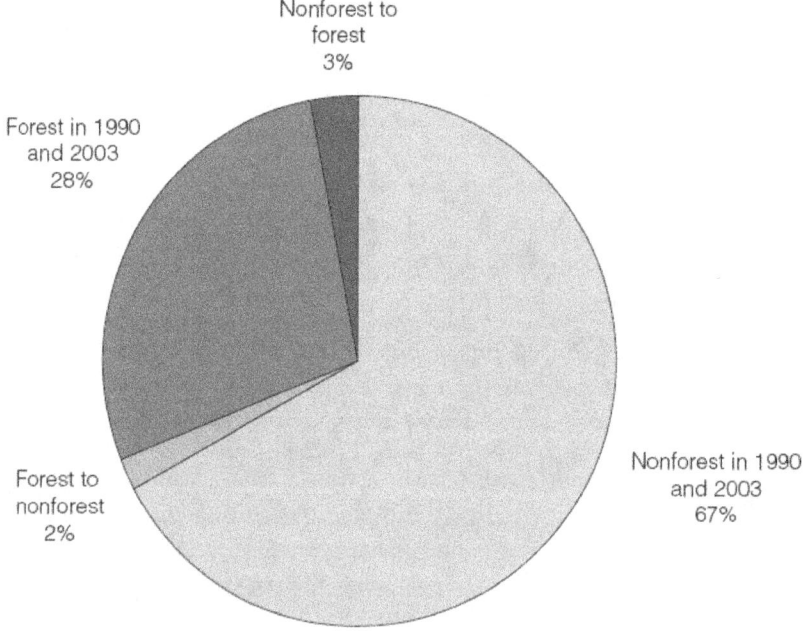

Figure 5.2. Forest land reversions by previous land use, Minnesota, 1990-2003.

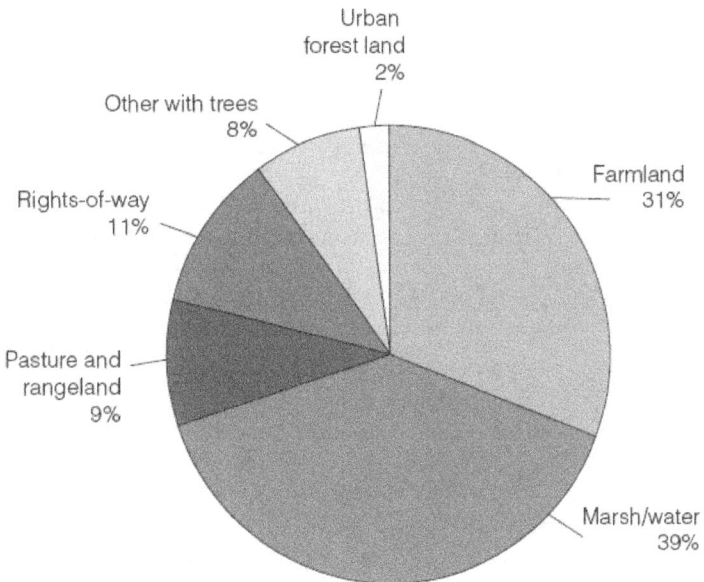

Figure 5.3. Forest land diversions by current land use, Minnesota, 1990-2003.

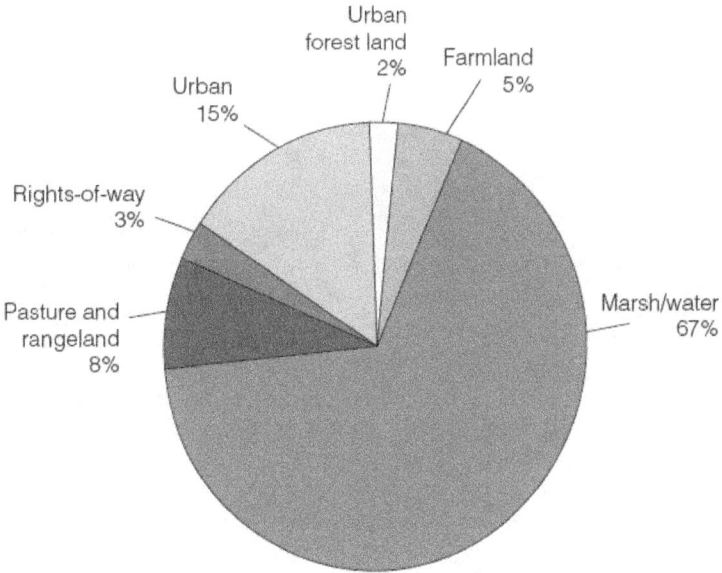

Nonindustrial Private Forest Landowners

Background:

The fate of Minnesota's forests lies predominantly in the hands of the people who own them and the organizations that administer them. In Minnesota, 56 percent of forest land is publicly administered. Nonindustrial private forest landowners (families and individuals) own 32 percent of Minnesota's forest land.

The goods and services produced and provided by forests are a function of forest land owners' objectives, opportunities, and constraints. Continued pressures from a changing society are altering how landowners choose to manage their forest land.

What We Found:

In 1982, an estimated 131 thousand owners held 5.1 million acres of private forest land (Carpenter 1986). By 2003, the number of private owners had swelled to an estimated 173 thousand families and individuals owning 5.3 million acres or 32 percent of Minnesota's forest land (Butler and Leatherberry 2004). The average landholding size decreased from 39 acres in 1982 to 31 acres in 2003. Most private landowners (82 percent) own fewer than 50 acres (fig 5.4). The 18 percent of private landowners who own 50 acres or more own 68 percent of the private forest land in Minnesota. Approximately 80 percent of the families, holding 88 percent of the non-industrial forest land, have owned it for more than 10 years.

The most common reasons for owning forest land include aesthetics, privacy, hunting and fishing, nature protection, family legacy, and other recreational uses. Harvesting trees for timber and firewood is a common activity of people who own 68 percent of family forest land. Harvesting of one kind or another occurred on 45 percent of ownerships within the past 5 years (fig. 5.5). Within the next 5 years, 43 percent of landowners intend to harvest firewood and 19 percent intend to harvest saw logs or pulpwood. Although 31 percent of forest land owners have sought forest management advice, only 17 percent have written management plans.

More than 30 percent of family landowners are 65 years or older, and 13 percent of forest land is owned by people who plan to pass some or all of their forest land on to heirs within the next 5 years.

What This Means:

The demographics of Minnesota's group of forest landowners has changed and will continue to do so. The process of parcelization, the dividing up of forest landholdings into smaller parcels, is likely to continue as long as land development pressures persist and incentives for maintaining working forest lands are not dramatically increased. The future land use intentions and age distributions of the owners indicate a large amount of forest land will soon be transferred to new owners. These new owners will offer new opportunities and challenges for those interested in the future of the forest resources of Minnesota.

Figure 5.4. Number of acres (thousands) and number of owners (hundreds) by size of owner land holdings, Minnesota, 2003. (Error bars represent one standard error.)

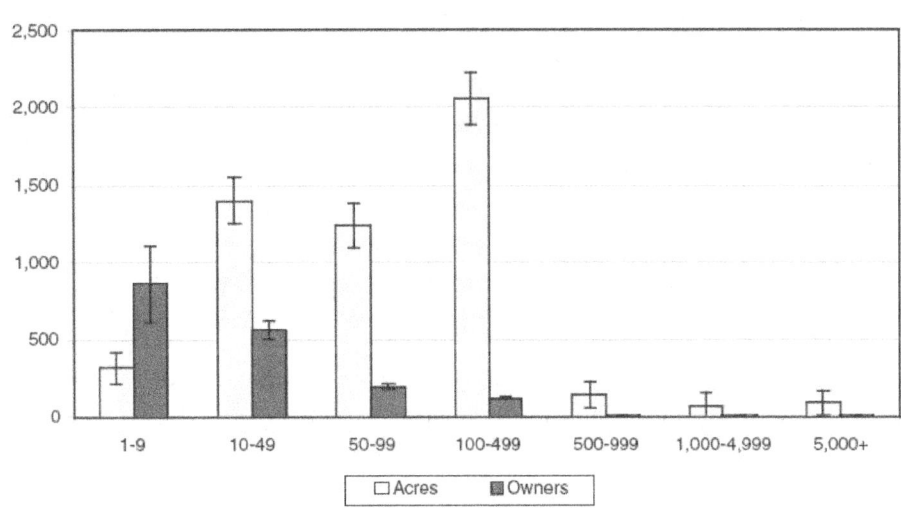

Figure 5.5. Area of family-owned forests in Minnesota by recent (past 5 years) forestry activity. (Error bars represent one standard error.)

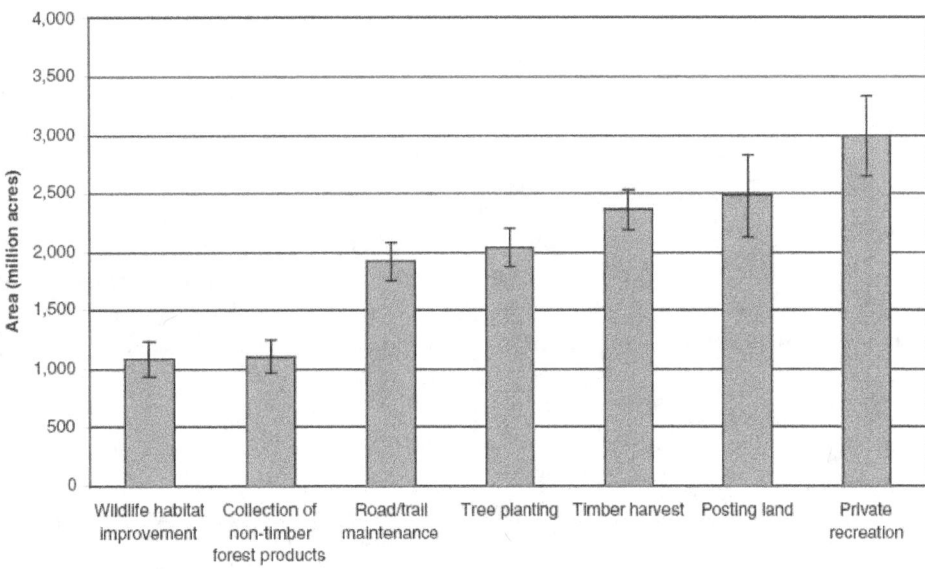

Forest Fragmentation and Parcelization

Background:

Forest fragmentation occurs when a contiguous forest area is divided into smaller blocks, through the construction of roads and housing, clearing for agriculture, or other human development. Fragmentation can also occur as a result of natural processes such as fire and flooding. Parcelization is the process by which large holdings by one owner are broken up into smaller holdings by multiple owners.

Fragmentation and parcelization of forest land areas have been identified as major issues in the United States. Preliminary findings from the 2002 U.S. timber assessment (Haynes 2003) indicate that approximately 15 to 20 million acres of U.S. forest land could be converted to urban and developed uses over the next 50 years. Such land use conversions could result from residential development in forested landscapes, as the U.S. population is estimated to grow by another 126 million people.

What We Found:

National Land Cover Dataset imagery (30 x 30 meter map pixels) for 1992 and 2001 (Vogelmann et al. 2001) was classified using techniques developed by Riitters et al. (2002) into classes of landscape pattern. Riitters et al. method was to classify map pixels based on the characteristics of each pixel and adjacent pixels (an area of approximately 6 acres). Pixels in mapping zone 41 of Minnesota, which includes all but the western and southernmost areas of the State, were classified into six forest pattern groups: interior forest (continuous forest canopy), edge (junction between forest and nonforest areas), perforated (nonforest patches in continuous forest areas), patch (small forest area surrounded by nonforest), transitional (about half of the cells in the surrounding area are forested) and nonforest. The proportion of pixels classified as interior forest decreased from 33 percent in 1992 to 25 percent in 2001 while the proportion of pixels in the perforated pattern increased from 11 percent to 18 percent over the same period (fig. 5.6). There were only minor changes in the proportion of pixels in edge, patch, transitional, and nonforest.

Some of the pixels classified as interior forest in 1992 were classified in a different pattern class in 2001 (fig. 5.7). Most pixels that were interior forest in 1992 (63 percent) remained interior forest in 2001. Of the 37 percent that changed classification, most (72 percent) were classed in the perforated landscape pattern in 2001. Forest interior areas decreased predominantly in the heavily forested areas of northern Minnesota (fig 5.8). To be considered interior forest, <u>all</u> the pixels in the 5x5 (pixel) analysis window have to be forest. With the large increase in nonforest pixels in 2001, this "moving analysis window" often included a nonforest pixel and, therefore, far fewer pixels could be classified as interior forest. When compared to the fragmentation map calculated from the 1992 National Land Cover Dataset (NLCD), there was a large loss of interior forest. This loss is largely due to the BWCAW blowdown, and although this area is still mostly forested, many of the pixels are now classified as edge, patch, transitional, or perforated rather than interior.

What This Means:

Based on map pixel analysis from 1992 and 2001, there is a trend of decreasing forest interior in zone 41 of Minnesota (fig. 5.8). The decrease in the total amount of interior forest in Minnesota indicates a possible negative trend in forest health. Although some wildlife species benefit from fragmentation and the resulting increase in forest edge, fragmentation can have adverse impacts on the forest including the loss of biodiversity, increased populations of invasive and nonnative species, changes in biotic and abiotic environments, changing landowner objectives, and decreased or more costly natural resources as in the case of timber management (Haynes 2003). Housing development is a major cause of habitat loss and fragmentation, due in part to new roads built to access homes (Radeloff et al. 2005a). From 1940 to 2000, housing increased by 146 percent in the Midwest (Radeloff et al. 2005b) and about one-third of this growth occurred in nonmetropolitan counties. Houses in nonmetropolitan areas tend to be more dispersed, causing higher levels of habitat loss and fragmentation per housing unit (Theobald et al. 1997).

Figure 5.6. Distribution of landscape patterns derived from National Land Cover Dataset classification in southern Minnesota for 1992 and 2001.

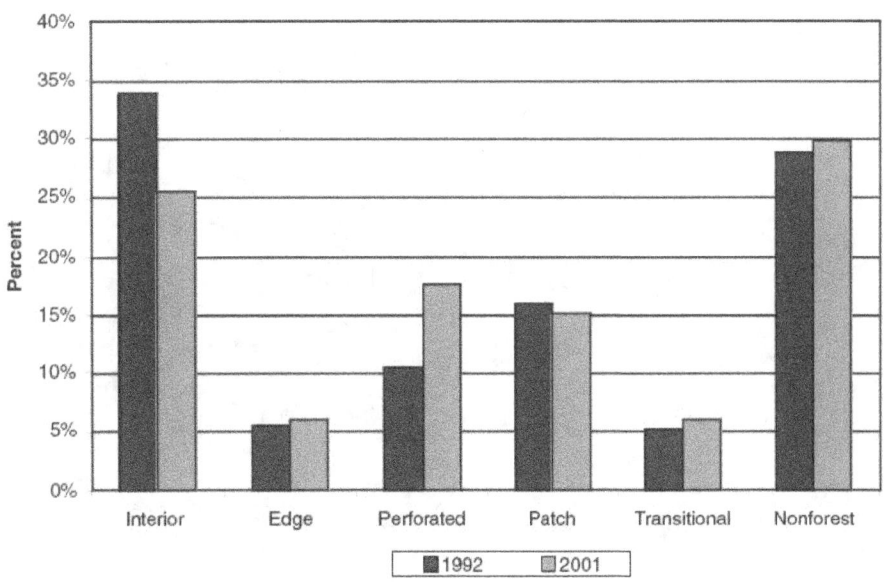

Figure 5.7. Current classification of pixels classified interior forest in 1992 but reclassified in 2001 as either edge, perforated, patch, transitional, or nonforest in Minnesota zone 41.

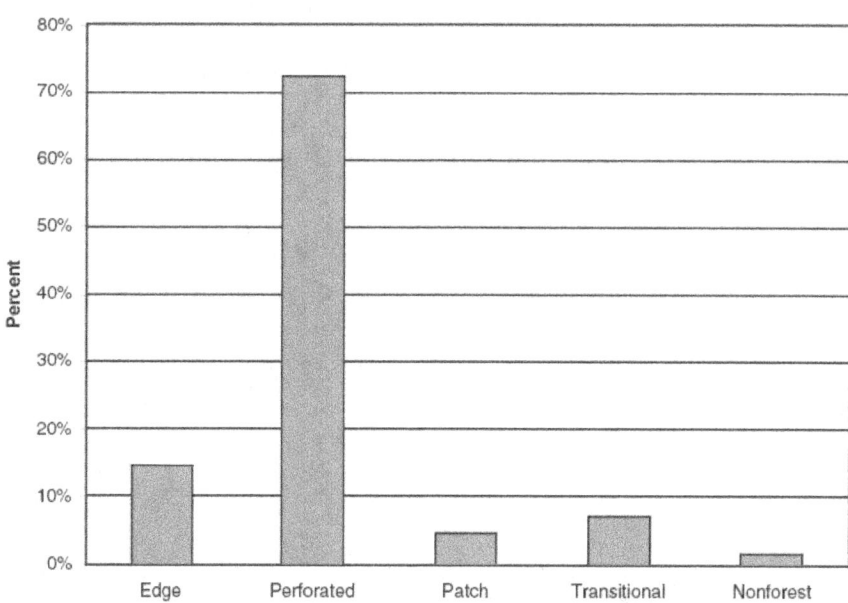

Figure 5.8. Landscape pattern changes, mapping zone 41, Minnesota, 1992-2001.

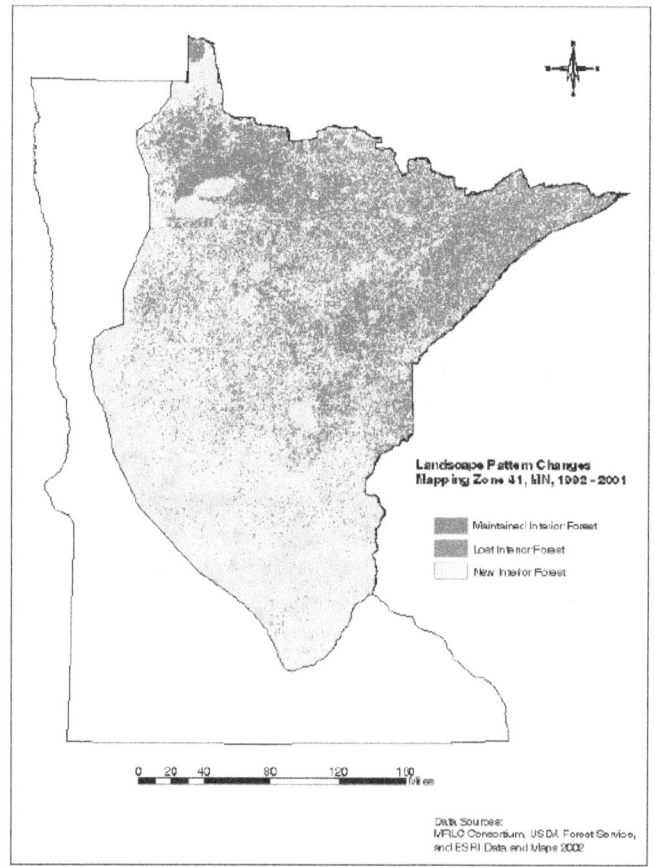

Nonnative and Invasive Plant Species

Background:

Introduced and invasive species can be detrimental to native forest ecosystems. Invasive species may displace native vegetation, sometimes dominating ecological niches previously occupied by native species, and reduce forest ecosystem diversity, resiliency, and wildlife habitat.

What We Found:

Information about trees obtained from 5,165 FIA field plots and information about understory vegetation obtained from 38 phase 3 plots (vegetative diversity) measured in 2003 (understory vegetation data for earlier years is not currently available) may be used to assess the prevalence of introduced and invasive plant species. A total of 283 species were identified on the 38 vegetative diversity plots. Eighteen of the 38 plots had at least one identifiable invasive or introduced species (http://www.nrs.fs.fed.us/fia/topics/invasives/manuals/) (fig. 5.9). Eighteen different invasive/introduced species were found on these 18 plots. Three plots had eight or more introduced or invasive species. The most prevalent invasive species was bird vetch, which occurred on five of the plots. Three of the plots had common buckthorn. Four invasive/introduced species occurred on two plots: bull thistle, glossy buckthorn, red clover, and garden vetch.

Several other species occurred on one plot: common St. Johnswort, white deadnettle, birdfoot deervetch, Virginia stock, black bindweed, marshpepper knotweed, cowslip primrose, nightflowering silene, common sowthistle, common chickweed, field pennycress, and golden clover.

The most common introduced tree species that occurs in the overstory is Siberian elm, which was often planted in windbreaks. Other introduced tree species include Scotch pine, Austrian pine, apple, larch, blue spruce, and a variety of poplars.

What This Means:

Based on the preliminary data, invasive or introduced species are likely found on about half the forests of Minnesota. The extent to which these introduced or invasive species cause harm cannot be assessed at this time; however, these species could potentially reduce the overall diversity and health of Minnesota's forests. Common buckthorn, in particular, has established itself on a significant number of plots surveyed by the vegetation diversity inventory, with 17 other species found on one or more of the 38 sample plots. Invasive or introduced species appear to occur on recently disturbed sites or nonforest boundary areas, where low stand densities allow for establishment of new species.

Invasive tree species make up less than one-tenth of 1 percent of the tree biomass in Minnesota. Still, over time, invasive species may displace native species and reduce the value and health of Minnesota's forests.

Paul Wray, Iowa State University

Figure 5.9. Number of introduced species found on vegetative diversity plots, Minnesota, 2003 (total of 38 plots in 2003).

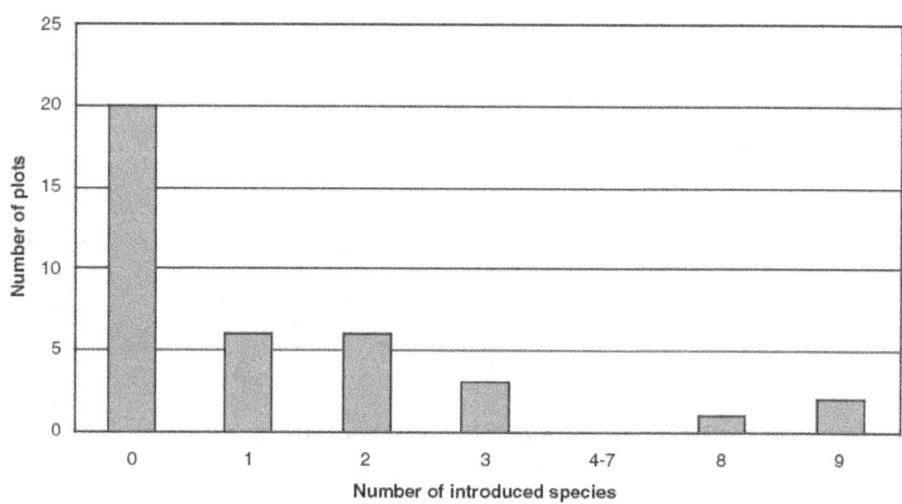

Wildlife Habitat

Background:

Habitat requirements vary by species. Some species require interior mature forests; other species require forest edge. Still others require both habitats at different times of the year or of their life cycle. Addressing habitat requirements by individual species is beyond the scope of this report. Broad characterizations of wildlife habitat using FIA data can be made, however, by looking at several indicators. Information from these indicators may also help to identify areas lacking adequate habitat while establishing a baseline of monitoring data. Mature forests, presence or absence of snags, quantity of coarse woody debris, and forest spatial patterns are all important descriptors of forest wildlife habitat.

What We Found:

Mature forests. Diverse stages of stand development are found across the forests of Minnesota (fig. 5.10). Generally, more mature forests (based on mean tree size and stand density assessments) are found in the prairie areas of Minnesota; younger stands are more typically found in the northern part of the State where removals are highest.

Standing-dead or snag trees are important habitat for birds and mammals. The downy woodpecker and 31 other Minnesota forest bird species rely on tree cavities and snags for feeding and nesting (Pfannmuller and Green 1999). Most cavity-nesting birds are insectivores and help to control the insect population. Additionally snags are used as a source of food by 26 mammal species and are a critical component of wildlife habitat (University of Minnesota Extension Service 2005).

The abundance of snags is highly variable across the forests of Minnesota, although the greatest amounts appear to occur in the northeastern part of the State probably due largely to the July 4, 1999, blowdown (fig. 5.11).

In Minnesota, for every 100 live trees more than 5 inches in diameter, there are 13 snag trees. For hardwoods, there are 12.6 snags per 100 live hardwoods; for softwoods, there are 13.7 snags per 100 live softwoods.

The ratio of standing dead to live trees is slightly higher in national forests (0.15) than in lands held by State and local governments (0.13) and private ownership (0.12). Part of the reason for this may be differences in stand age. The average stand age is 57 years for national forests, 55 years for State and local government land, and 52 years for private land.

The largest quantities of coarse woody debris are found in areas affected by wind disturbances. Most recently these areas include the BWCAW and prairie border forests.

What This Means:

Current inventory data indicate diverse and abundant forest habitat (snags, coarse woody debris, and forest patterns) to support numerous wildlife species across Minnesota. However, data are insufficient to project trends or draw conclusions about individual wildlife species. For species that depend on continuous forest cover in mature forests, there is evidence that the area of mature forest is increasing across Minnesota but that the area of interior forests has decreased. For species that require both the cover of mature forests and foraging areas of nonforest environments, the continued maturation and fragmentation of Minnesota's forests will maintain these habitat intermixes.

Figure 5.10. Proportion (interpolated) of forest land in large-diameter stands, Minnesota, 2003.

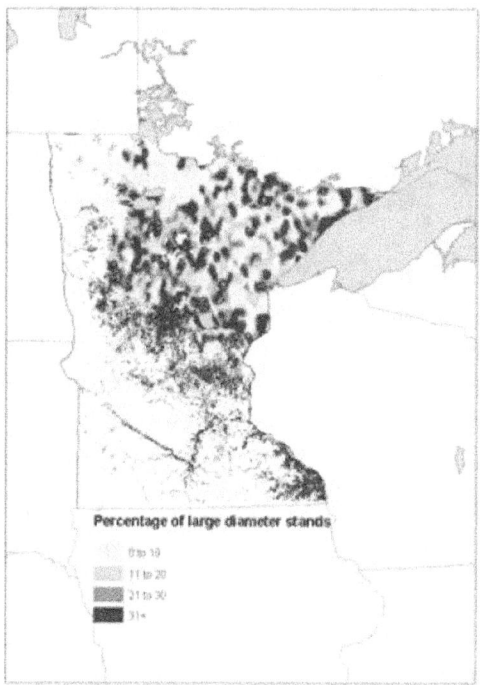

Figure 5.11. Number (interpolated) of standing dead trees as a percent of standing live and dead trees, Minnesota, 2003.

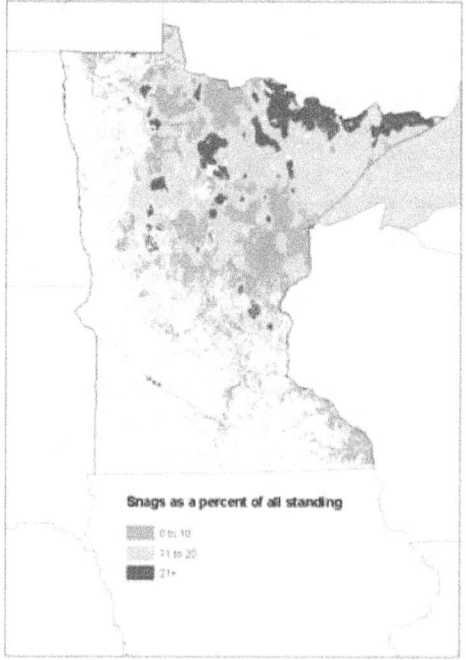

Exotic Pests

European Gypsy Moth

Background:

The European gypsy moth has been slowly moving westward since it was accidentally introduced into Massachusetts in 1869. Over the past 25 years, Minnesota has successfully eliminated more than 30 infestations, but eventually the moths will become established. Of special concern was the identification of two egg masses in the fall of 2004 near the town of Tower and only 1 mile south of the Boundary Waters Canoe Area (Cremers 2004).

What We Found:

Once the gypsy moth is established, the most important factor affecting a forest's susceptibility to defoliation is the proportion of the forest made up of tree species that gypsy moth caterpillars prefer to eat. Preferred species include the oaks, aspen, basswood, paper birch, and tamarack (Barnacle and Burks 2005) and are found on 85 percent of Minnesota's forest land. Less preferred are yellow birch, box elder, walnut, spruce, cottonwood, red and sugar maples, and pine. The gypsy moth caterpillars avoid ash, red cedar, balsam fir, and silver maple. Stands dominated by preferred species are defoliated at higher rates, more often, and for longer periods of time than stands composed of avoided species.

What This Means:

Site conditions and individual tree vigor play a role in how many defoliated trees die. Only a portion of those trees defoliated are at risk of mortality. When gypsy moths become established in Minnesota and defoliate large areas, the repeated defoliation and tree mortality will likely shift susceptible stand composition away from oaks and other preferred species toward nonpreferred species. On nutrient-rich sites, species such as red maple, sugar maple, and green ash may replace lost oaks. On drier, nutrient-poor sites, where seed sources occur, red and white pines may replace the oaks. In northern Minnesota, the number of balsam fir will likely increase (Barnacle and Burks 2005).

Emerald Ash Borer

Background:

The emerald ash borer (EAB), an exotic insect pest native to Asia, was detected in Michigan in 2002. Larvae feed in the cambium between the bark and wood, producing galleries that eventually girdle and kill branches and entire trees. Evidence suggests that EAB has been established in Michigan for at least 6 to 10 years. More than 3 thousand square miles in southeast Michigan are infested, and more than 5 million ash trees are dead or dying from this pest (McCullough and Katovich 2004). This exotic pest is also established in Windsor, Ontario, and has been identified in northeast Indiana. Some forest entomologists believe EAB could have a greater impact on the Nation's cities and forests than gypsy moth.

What We Found:

Although the EAB has not been identified in Minnesota, it is probably just a matter of time before it is. Forestry personnel consider all forest areas containing ash trees across the State and region to be at risk for infestation and the loss of the ash component. Therefore, identifying areas containing ash, determining ash seedling/sapling amounts, and determining the ratio of ash to non-ash resources is crucial to assessing and mitigating the potential impact of EAB in the future.

Ash trees make up 7 percent of the total all-live volume on Minnesota's forest land. Ash trees are well distributed across Minnesota (fig 5.12). Ash is a component of nearly 3.8 million acres of Minnesota forest land. It constitutes the majority of all-live volume in a stand on 902 thousand acres and at least 25 percent of the stand volume on 1.5 million acres of forest land.

What This Means:

If the emerald ash borer were to kill all ash trees across Minnesota, 23 percent of Minnesota's forests would be affected. Most often only a minority of trees would be killed in any stand. If EAB became a persistent pest, ash regeneration would be significantly reduced in time because the mature ash trees would no longer be present to provide seeds. Thus, EAB could eliminate or severely reduce the ash component of many forests, similar to the impact of Dutch elm disease on Minnesota's forests.

Figure 5.12. All-live tree volume of ash on forest land, Minnesota, 2003.

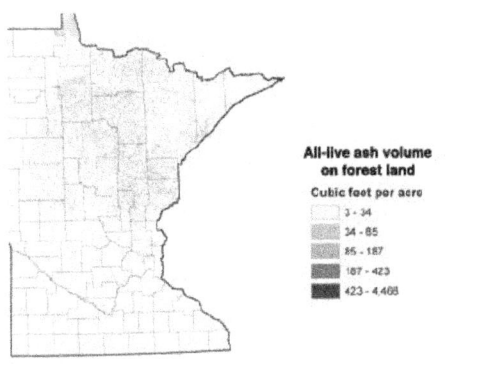

Forest Products

Forest Products

Timber Product Output

Timber harvesting produces economic benefits for persons involved in timber ownership, management, marketing, harvesting, hauling, and distribution to processing mills. Approximately 29,200 people are employed in primary processing (including logging) and 24,000 are employed in secondary manufacturing. Total payroll for the forest products sector of the Minnesota forest economy is estimated at $1.9 billion (10 percent of all manufacturing in Minnesota). The value of forest products manufacturing shipments was estimated at $6.48 billion in 2002 (Minnesota Forest Industries).

The key sectors of the forest products industry include sawmills, pulp and particleboard (flakeboard, waferboard, oriented strandboard, and medium-density fiberboard) mills, and secondary processors.

Most primary processing takes place in northeastern Minnesota where the majority of the timber resource is located. Of the eight pulp mills in Minnesota, five produce paper: UPM-Kymenne (Grand Rapids), Boise (International Falls), International Paper (International Falls), Stora Enso (Duluth), and Sappi Fine Paper Company (Cloquet). Three mills specialize in hardboard and specialty products Certainteed Corporation (Shakopee), International Bildrite (International Falls), and Georgia-Pacific Corp. Superwood Division (Duluth).

Minnesota's oriented strand board (OSB) and engineered wood products industry is also located in the north. OSB plants are located in Grand Rapids (Ainsworth Lumber), Two Harbors (Louisiana-Pacific), Bemidji (Ainsworth Lumber and Northwood Panelboard), and Cook (Ainsworth Lumber). A laminated strand board plant is located in Deerwood (Trus Joist, a Weyerhaeuser Business).

Minnesota produced nearly 3.0 million cords of pulpwood (including mill residues) in 2002 (Piva 2005). Pulpwood includes all fiber-based products made from roundwood including particleboard, OSB, waferboard, and engineered lumber. Aspen roundwood accounted for 68 percent of the roundwood used for pulpwood production; 11 percent came from other hardwoods, and 21 percent came from softwoods.

The eight pulp mills, five OSB mills, and one laminated structural lumber mill in Minnesota reported consuming almost 3.6 million cords in 2002, an increase of 10 percent from 2001. Minnesota's pulp and particleboard mills acquired 19 percent of their raw material from out-of-State sources. More than 50 percent of the imported wood material came from Wisconsin, and most of the rest came from Canada.

More than 278 million cubic feet of industrial roundwood was harvested for the primary wood-using industry from Minnesota's forest land in 2003. Aspen accounted for 55 percent of the total harvest. Jack pine, white birch, and spruce were other important species, but combined they made up only 22 percent of the total harvest. Pulpwood was the major product harvested, accounting for 80 percent of the total harvest. Saw logs were the other major forest product, with 19 percent of the harvest. Other products harvested were veneer, excelsior and shavings bolts, poles and posts, cabin logs, and other miscellaneous products.

Almost 95 percent of the industrial roundwood harvested in Minnesota was processed by Minnesota mills. Of the 278 million cubic feet of industrial roundwood produced, 95 percent came from growing-stock sources. The remainder of the industrial roundwood came from cull trees, limbwood, dead trees, and saplings.

In the process of harvesting industrial roundwood from Minnesota's forest land, 16 million cubic feet of growing-stock material and 127 million cubic feet of non-growing-stock material were left on the ground as logging residue and slash. Non-growing-stock sources of industrial roundwood contain greater volumes of unusable material, thus the much greater volume of logging slash as compared to growing stock.

Timber Assessment: 50-year Projections

Background:

The Forest Rangeland Renewable Resource Planning Act of 1974 (RPA 1974) directs the USDA Forest Service to conduct periodic assessments of the condition of all forest and rangeland resources in the United States. In addition to reporting on the current status of the resource, the assessment identifies prospective changes in the land and timber resource base, estimates the major determinants of trends in demand and supply, and examines the implications of these trends in making 50-year projections of the U.S. forest sector. The model used for the inventory projections is known as the aggregate timberland assessment system (ATLAS; Mills and Kincaid 1992). The "... economic assumptions are grouped according to their relation to the demand (consumption) and supply (or production) aspects of the assessment. Demand assumptions include macroeconomic activity; pulp and paper, the context for trade; and fuelwood demand. Supply assumptions include land use, area of timberland, investment in land management by different owners, adjustments for timber removals, and harvest from public timberlands." A complete list of assumptions used in developing these projections can be found in chapter 2 of "An Analysis of the Timber Situation in the United States: 1952 to 2050" (Haynes 2003).

The projections used in the national report were made at the county level and then aggregated to multistate reporting units. The projections displayed in this report are based on the same county-level projections used in the national report.

What Was Projected:

The area of timberland in Minnesota is projected to decrease over the next 50 years (fig. 6.1) from 14.8 million acres in 2003 to 13.4 million acres in 2060. Growing-stock volumes on timberland are expected to increase over the same period from 15.3 billion cubic feet to 26.9 billion cubic feet.

Average annual net growth is projected to range from 417 million to 457 million cubic feet over 2010 to 2050, about 85 percent above the projected average annual removals range of 219 million to 257 million cubic feet (fig. 6.2). Expressed in terms of standing volume, however, the growth rate will decline from 2.5 percent of the growing-stock volume in 2010 to 1.7 percent of the growing-stock volume in 2050. The removals rate will likewise decline from 1.3 percent of the growing-stock volume in 2010 to 0.8 percent of the growing-stock volume in 2050.

What This Means:

The area of timberland is projected to continue to decline over the next 50 years in response to increasing population pressures and economic pressure to use the land in a different way. While the area of timberland is projected to decrease by approximately 10 percent over the next 50 years, the volume of growing stock is expected to increase by approximately 76 percent over the same period. The volume per acre is projected to nearly double over the next five decades, increasing from 1,035 cubic feet/acre in 2003 to 2,003 cubic feet/acre in 2060.

Figure 6.1. Projected area of timberland and cubic foot volume of growing stock, Minnesota, 2003 through 2060.

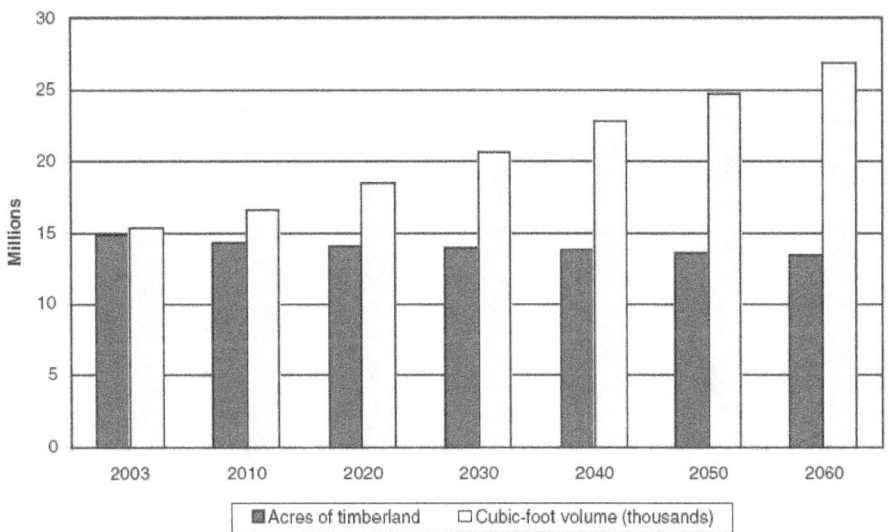

Figure 6.2. Projected average annual net cubic foot growth of growing stock and average annual cubic foot removals of growing stock, Minnesota, 2003 through 2050.

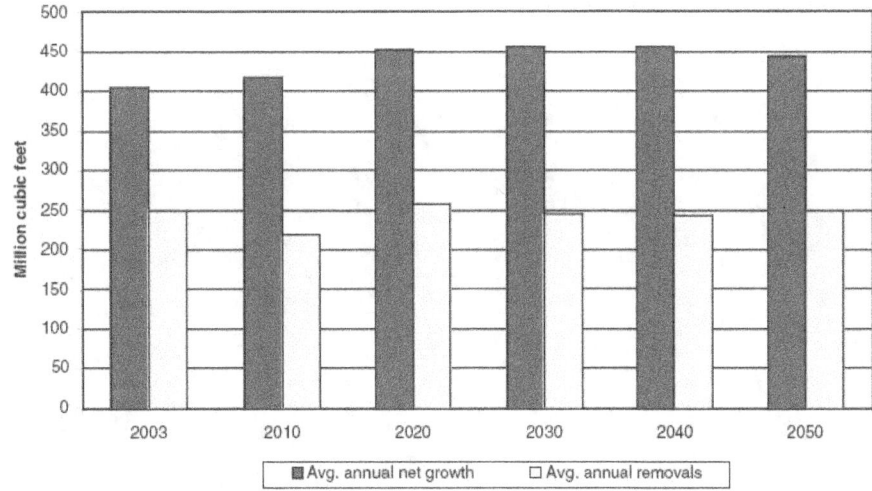

Data Sources and Techniques

Data Sources and Techniques

Forest Inventory

The North Central[4] Research Station's Forest Inventory and Analysis (NCFIA) program began fieldwork for the 12th forest inventory of Minnesota's forest resources in 1999. This launched the new annual inventory system in which one-fifth of the field plots (considered one panel) are measured each year. In 2003, NCFIA completed measurement of the fifth and final panel of inventory plots in Minnesota. Now that all panels have been measured, each will be remeasured approximately every 5 years. Previous inventories of Minnesota's forest resources were completed in 1935, 1953, 1962, 1977, and 1990 (Zon 1935, Cunningham et al. 1958, Stone 1966, Jakes 1980, Leatherberry et al. 1995).

Data from new inventories are often compared with data from earlier inventories to determine trends in forest resources. However, for the comparisons to be valid, the procedures used in the two inventories must be similar. As a result of our ongoing efforts to improve the efficiency and reliability of the inventory, several changes in procedures and definitions have been made since the last Minnesota inventory in 1990 (Miles et al. 1995). Although these changes will have little effect on statewide estimates of forest area, timber volume, and tree biomass, they may significantly affect plot classification variables such as forest type and stand-size class. Estimates of growth, removals, and mortality were based on the partial remeasurement of variable-radius subplots measured during the 1990 inventory. Current volume was established on fixed-radius plots. Although these changes allow limited comparison of inventory estimates among separate inventories in this report, it is inappropriate to directly compare all portions of the 1999-2003 data with those published for earlier inventories.

The 1999-2003 Minnesota forest inventory was done in three phases. During the first phase, FIA used a computer-assisted classification of satellite imagery to form two initial strata—forest and nonforest. Pixels within 60 m (2 pixel widths) of a forest/nonforest edge formed two additional strata—forest/nonforest and nonforest/forest. Forest pixels within 60 m of a forest/nonforest boundary on the forest side were classified into a forest edge stratum. Pixels within 60 m of the boundary on the nonforest side were classified into a nonforest edge stratum. The estimated population total for a variable is the sum across all strata of the product of each stratum's estimated area and the variable's estimated mean per unit area for the stratum.

The second phase of the forest inventory consisted of the actual field measurements. Current FIA precision standards for annual inventories require a sampling intensity of one plot for approximately every 6,000 acres. The entire area of the United States has been divided into nonoverlapping hexagons, each containing 5,937 acres (McRoberts 1999). The total Federal base sample of plots has been systematically divided into five interpenetrating, nonoverlapping subsamples or panels. Each year the plots in a single panel are measured, and panels are selected on a 5-year, rotating basis (McRoberts 1999). For estimation purposes, the measurement of each panel of plots may be considered an independent systematic sample of all land in a State. Field crews measured vegetation on plots forested at the time of the last inventory and on plots currently classified as forest by trained photointerpreters using aerial photos or digital orthoquads. The State of Minnesota contributed resources to allow field crews to survey twice as many phase 2 plots.

---

[4] *Now the Northern Research Station, NRS-FIA.*

NCFIA has two categories of field plot measurements—phase 2 field plots (standard FIA plots) and phase 3 plots (forest health plots)—to optimize our ability to collect data when available for measurement. A suite of tree and site attributes are measured on phase 2 plots, and a full suite of forest health variables are measured on phase 3 plots. Both types of plots are uniformly distributed both geographically and temporally. The 1999-2003 annual inventory results represent field measures on 5,165 phase 2 forested plots and 267 phase 3 forested plots.

The overall phase 2 plot layout consists of four subplots. The centers of subplots 2, 3, and 4 are located 120 feet from the center of subplot 1. The azimuths to subplots 2, 3, and 4 are 0, 120, and 240 degrees, respectively. Trees with a d.b.h. 5 inches and larger are measured on a 24-foot-radius (1/24 acre) circular subplot. All trees less than 5 inches d.b.h. are measured on a 6.8-foot-radius (1/300 acre) circular microplot located 12 feet east of the center of each of the four subplots. Forest conditions that occur on any of the four subplots are recorded. Factors that differentiate forest conditions are changes in forest type, stand-size class, land use, ownership, and density. For details on the sample protocols for phase 2 variables and all phase 3 indicators, please refer to http://fia.fs.fed.us/library/fact-sheets/.

Timber Products Output Inventory

This study was a cooperative effort of the Division of Forestry of the Minnesota Department of Natural Resources (MN DNR) and the North Central Research Station (NCRS). Using a questionnaire designed to determine the size and composition of Minnesota's forest products industry, its use of roundwood, and its generation and disposition of wood residues, Minnesota Division of Forestry personnel visited all known primary wood-using mills within the State. Completed questionnaires were sent to NCRS for editing and processing. As part of data editing and processing, all industrial roundwood volumes reported on the questionnaires were converted to standard units of measure using regional conversion factors. Timber removals by source of material and harvest residues generated during logging were estimated from standard product volumes using factors developed from logging utilization studies previously conducted by NCRS.

National Woodland Landowner Survey

This survey of private woodland owners is conducted annually by the USDA Forest Service to help us better understand owner demographics and motivation. Every year questionnaires are mailed to individuals and private groups who own woodlands where FIA has established forest inventory plots. Twenty percent of these ownerships (about 50,000) are contacted each year; more detailed questionnaires are sent out in years that end in 2 or 7 to coincide with national census, inventory, and assessment programs.

National Land Cover Data Imagery

Derived from Landsat Thematic Mapper satellite data (30-m pixel), the National Land Cover Dataset (NLCD) is a land cover classification scheme (21 classes) applied across the United States by the U.S. Geological Survey (USGS) and the U.S. Environmental Protection Agency (EPA). The NLCD was developed from data acquired by the Multi-Resolution Land Characterization (MRLC) Consortium, a partnership of Federal agencies that produce or use land cover data. Partners include the USGS, EPA, USDA Forest Service, and National Oceanic and Atmospheric Administration.

Mapping Procedures

Maps in this report were constructed by either (1) categorical coloring of Minnesota counties (based on the 2000 U.S. Census) or hexagons (obtained from the EPA Ecological Mapping and Assessment Program) according to forest attributes (such as forest land area) or (2) the interpolation of forest attributes using inverse distance weighting techniques and masking out nonforest land using NLCD imagery. Because the forest inventory is based on plot data collected at distinct points, inferences must be drawn about the entirety of Minnesota's forests. Interpolation between plot locations allows creation of forest attribute maps that display continuous spatial estimates. Inverse Distance Weighting (IDW), which assumes that things close to one another are more alike than those farther apart, is the interpolation method employed in this report. To predict a value for any unmeasured location, IDW uses the measured values surrounding the prediction location. This assumes each measured point has a local influence that diminishes with distance, thus the term "inverse distance weighting." For more information, see Johnston et al. (2001).

A variation of the k-nearest-neighbor (KNN) technique was used to apply information from forest inventory plots to remotely sensed Modis imagery based on the spectral characterization of pixels and additional geospatial information to produce a forest type map (fig. 2.3), an all-live tree volume map (fig. 3.5), a percent softwood volume map (fig. 3.8), a quaking aspen volume map (fig 3.10) and an ash volume map (fig. 5.12).

References

Amacher, M.C.; O'Neill, K.P. [In prep.]. *Soil vital signs: a new index for assessing forest soil health.*

Anderson, J.L.; Bell, J.C.; Cooper, T.H.; Grigal, D.F. 2001. *Soils and landscapes of Minnesota.* St. Paul, MN: University of Minnesota Extension Service. [Available online at: http://www.extension.umn.edu/distribution/cropsystems/DC2331.html]

Bailey, R.G. 1976. *Description of the ecoregions of the United States.* Fort Collins, CO: U.S. Department of Agriculture, Forest Service. [Available online at: http://www.fs.fed.us/land/ecosysmgmt/ecoreg1_home.html]

Barnacle, W.; Burks, S. 2005. *Minimizing gypsy moth.* Minnesota Department of Natural Resources. [Available online at: http://www.dnr.state.mn.us/treecare/forest_health/gypsy-moth/minimizedamage.html]

Belcher, David M.; Holdaway, Margaret R.; Brand, Gary J. 1982. *A description of STEMS—the stand and tree evaluation and modeling system.* Gen. Tech. Rep. NC-79. St. Paul, MN: U.S. Department of Agriculture, Forest Service, North Central Forest Experiment Station. 18 p.

Bohlen, P.J.; Groffman, P.M.; Fahey, T.J.; et al. 2004a. *Ecosystem consequences of exotic earthworm invasion in north temperate forests.* Ecosystems. 7(1): 1-12.

Bohlen, P.J.; Scheu, S.; Hale, C.M.; et al. 2004b. *Non-native invasive earthworms as agents of change in northern temperate forests.* Frontiers in Ecology and Environment. 2(8): 427-435.

Brady, N.C. 1990. *The nature and properties of soils.* 10th ed. New York, NY: Macmillan. 621 p.

Butler, J.B.; Leatherberry, E.C. 2004. *America's family forest owners.* Journal of Forestry. 102(7): 4-14.

Carpenter, E.M.; Hansen, M.H.; St. John, D.M. 1986. *The private forest landowners of Minnesota - 1982.* Resour. Bull. NC-95. St. Paul, MN: U.S. Department of Agriculture, Forest Service, North Central Forest Experiment Station. 55 p.

Cremers, K.T. 2004. *Minnesota Department of Natural Resources Forest Insect & Disease Newsletter - December 2004.* [Available online at: http://www.dnr.state.mn.us/fid/dec04/feature.html]

Cunningham, R.N.; Horn, A.G.; Quinney, D.N. 1958. *Minnesota's forest resources, 1958.* For. Resour. Rep. 13. St. Paul, MN: U.S. Department of Agriculture, Forest Service, Lake States Forest Experiment Station. 53 p.

Gundale, M.J. 2002. *Influence of exotic earthworms on the soil organic horizon and the rare fern Botrychium mormo.* Conservation Biology. 16(6): 1555-1561.

Hale, C.M.; Frelich L.E.; Reich P.B. 2005. *Exotic European earthworm invasion dynamics in northern hardwood forests of Minnesota, USA*. Ecological Applications. 15(3): 848-860.

Hahn, J.T. 1984. *Tree volume and biomass equations for the Lake States*. Res. Pap. NC-250. St. Paul, MN: U.S. Department of Agriculture, Forest Service, North Central Forest Experiment Station. 10 p.

Haynes, R.H., tech. coord. 2003. *An analysis of the timber situation in the United States: 1952 to 2050*. Gen. Tech. Rep. PNW-560. Portland, OR: U.S. Department of Agriculture, Forest Service, Pacific Northwest Research Station. 254 p.

Jacobson, K.L. 2004. *Minnesota forest resources*. September 2004. Minnesota Department of Natural Resources, Division of Forestry. [Available online at: http://files.dnr.state.mn.us/forestry/um/2004mn_forest_resources.pdf]

Jakes, P.J. 1980. *The fourth Minnesota forest inventory: area*. Resour. Bull. NC-54. St. Paul, MN: U.S. Department of Agriculture, Forest Service, North Central Forest Experiment Station. 37 p.

Johnston, K.; Ver Hoef, J.M.; Krivoruchko, K.; Lucas, N. 2001. *Using ArcGIS geostatistical analyst*. Redlands, CA: ESRI. 300 p.

Leatherberry, E.C.; Spencer, J.S., Jr.; Schmidt, T.L.; Carroll, M.R. 1995. *An analysis of Minnesota's fifth forest resources inventory, 1990*. Resour. Bull. NC-165. St. Paul, MN: U.S. Department of Agriculture, Forest Service, North Central Forest Experiment Station. 102 p.

Marschner, F.J. 1930. Bureau of Agricultural Economics. Map derived from General Land Office field notes.

McBride, M.B. 1994. *Environmental chemistry of soils*. New York, NY: Oxford University Press. 406 p.

McCullough, D.G.; Katovich, S.A. 2004. *Pest alert: Emerald Ash Borer*. NA-PR-02-04. St. Paul, MN: U.S. Department of Agriculture, Forest Service, Northeastern Area, State and Private Forestry. n.p.

McRoberts, R.E. 1999. *Joint annual forest inventory and monitoring system, the North Central perspective*. Journal of Forestry. 97(12): 27-31.

MFRC. *Minnesota Forest Resources Council Web site*. [Available only online at: http://www.frc.state.mn.us/FMgdline/Guidelines.html] Accessed August 18, 2005.

Miles, Patrick D.; Chen, Chung M.; Leatherberry, Earl C. 1995. *Minnesota forest statistics, 1990, revised*. Resour. Bull. NC-158. St. Paul, MN: U.S. Department of Agriculture, Forest Service, North Central Forest Experiment Station. 138 p.

Mills, J.R.; Kincaid, J.C. 1992. *The aggregate timberland assessment system—ATLAS: a comprehensive timber projection model.* Gen. Tech. Rep. PNW-281. Portland, OR: U.S. Department of Agriculture, Forest Service, Pacific Northwest Research Station. 160 p.

Pfannmuller, L.A.; Green, J.C. 1999. *Birds and forests.* St. Paul, MN: Minnesota Conservation Volunteer March-April 1999.

Piva, R.J. 2005. *Pulpwood production in the North-Central region, 2002.* Resour. Bull. NC-239. St. Paul, MN: U.S. Department of Agriculture, Forest Service, North Central Research Station. 56 p.

Pritchett, W.L.; Fisher, R.F. 1987. *Properties and management of forest soils.* 2d ed. New York, NY: Wiley.

Radeloff, V.C.; Hammer, R.B.; Stewart, S.I.; et al. 2005a. *The wildland urban interface in the United States.* Ecological Applications. 15: 799-805.

Radeloff, V.C.; Hammer, R.B.; Stewart, S.I. 2005b. *Sprawl and forest fragmentation in the U.S. Midwest from 1940 to 2000.* Conservation Biology. 19: 793-805.

Raile, G.K. 1982. *Estimating stump volume.* Res. Pap. NC-224. St.Paul, MN: U.S. Department of Agriculture, Forest Service, North Central Forest Experiment Station. 4 p.

Riitters, K.H.; Wickham, J.D.; O'Neill, R.V.; et al. 2002. *Fragmentation of continental United States forests.* Ecosystems. 5: 815-822.

Smith, W.B. 1991. *Assessing removals for North Central forest inventories.* Res. Pap. NC-299. St. Paul, MN: U.S. Department of Agriculture, Forest Service, North Central Forest Experiment Station. 48 p.

Stone, R.N. 1966. *A third look at Minnesota's timber.* Resour. Bull. NC-1. St. Paul, MN: U.S. Department of Agriculture, Forest Service, North Central Forest Experiment Station. 70 p.

Theobald, D.M.; Miller, J.R.; Hobbs, N.T. 1997. *Estimating the cumulative effects of development on wildlife habitat.* Landscape and Urban Planning. 39: 25-36.

U.S. Department of Agriculture, Forest Products Laboratory. 1999. *Wood handbook— wood as an engineering material.* Gen. Tech. Rep. FPL-113. Madison, WI: U.S. Department of Agriculture, Forest Service, Forest Products Laboratory. 463 p.

University of Minnesota Extension Service, 2005. Bulletin-06340. Communication and Educational Technology Services. [Available online at: http://www.extension.umn.edu/distribution/youthdevelopment/components/6340-04.html]

U.S. Department of Agriculture, Natural Resources Conservation Service. 1999. *Soil taxonomy: a basic system of soil classification for making and interpreting soil surveys.* 2d ed. Agric. Handb. 436. Washington, DC: U.S. Department of Agriculture, Natural Resources Conservation Service.

Vogelmann, J.E.; Howard, S.M.; Yang, L.; et al. 2001. *Completion of the 1990s National Land Cover Dataset for the conterminous United States from Landsat Thematic Mapper data and ancillary data sources.* Photogrammetric Engineering and Remote Sensing. 67: 650-662.

Waters, T. 1977. *The streams and rivers of Minnesota.* Minneapolis, MN: University of Minnesota Press. 373 p.

Zon, R. 1935. *Economic notes: preliminary statistics and analysis of data obtained from forest surveys and other economic studies by the Lake States Forest Experiment Station.* For. Surv. 1. St. Paul, MN: University Farm. n.p.